roots for kids

A Genealogy Guide for Young People

Susan Provost Beller

2nd Edition

Copyright © 2007 by Susan Provost Beller
All Rights Reserved
First Edition 1989
Second Edition 2007
Published by Genealogical Publishing Company
3600 Clipper Mill Road, Suite 260, Baltimore, MD 21211

Library of Congress Catalogue Card Number 2007923230
International Standard Book Number 978-0-8063-1777-9
Made in the United States of America

Illustrations by Susan Riley and James Allen

*This book is dedicated to my husband, W. Michael
Beller, who always said I should write it,
to my three children, Michael Patrick, Jennie, and
Sean, who grew up thinking that everyone had
their picnics in cemeteries,
and to all those Beller and Provost ancestors
whose "stories" made genealogy impossible to resist.*

Introduction to the Second Edition

When I wrote *Roots for Kids* back in 1988, it was typed on a Commodore 64 computer. Each chapter had to be submitted separately due to the large size of each file, which that computer couldn't hold in its memory. Back then, I also had to do any talking with my editor or publisher either by phone or letter. I have had eight computers since then. And I now can communicate with an editor by Instant Messenger if I want to. I have even written and edited whole books right up to final galley proofs without them ever being printed out on paper.

The changes in computers and the amazing number of resources available on the Internet mean that it is time to update some of the information in this book. What does not change at all is the need to start with your own family. The types of records from the past have not changed either. What has changed is how we can access that material.

Young researchers can now use online databases without ever leaving their homes. They can access services like Ancestry.com online through their local library. This is wonderful for researching family history. However, it also means there's yet another kind of information that we have to check out carefully. The same Internet that gives us great family trees can also cause one mistake to be repeated by hundreds of people.

It is time to go back and see how young researchers can use this great new tool and still be good historians at the same time.

Preface

In April 1987, I had the pleasure of taking my genealogy enrichment class of six students to Vital Records and the Vermont Historical Society Library in Montpelier, Vermont. Over the years I had given many mini genealogy sessions to stir up kids' interest in genealogy and have them create a pedigree chart based on sources of information from relatives. I had also taught nine different genealogy courses for adults at various times. However, this was the first time I had done a complete course for kids that included two field trips to use the available resources. The people I had approached about bringing in six fourth- to sixth-graders had been somewhat reluctant. As the morning of our eagerly awaited visit dawned, I was also having my doubts.

Throughout the day a steady stream of visitors came to observe these "kids" doing genealogy. The students were serious about their research. They were knowledgeable about the materials they were using. They handled materials with the proper respect and care. The day was a fantastic success for everyone involved.

The course had been difficult to prepare due to a lack of materials at a level appropriate for the young reader. That need led directly to this book. It is an attempt to transfer my twelve-week class onto paper. Each chapter represents one forty-five minute class session, with homework assignments and class handout information included.

This material can be used in three ways:

1. As a twelve-week enrichment class in genealogy for grades four and up.

2. As a four- to five-week mini course in which students create a family tree based on home sources of information. Many social studies teachers have their students create a family tree, and this book offers a methodical introduction for best achieving the desired results.

3. As a self-taught genealogy course for grades six and up. A student user can work through the course one lesson at a time, developing his or her own family tree and continuing research on the Internet.

I hope that from this book the students will obtain an understanding of and an interest in genealogical research. It is also my firm hope that each will decide to find the stories hiding in his or her own history.

Contents

An Introduction to Genealogy

Have you ever done one of those really big jigsaw puzzles—the kind with about a zillion pieces? If you have, you know that each of the pieces of the puzzle doesn't give you much of the picture. You can tell that a certain piece is part of the sky or the ground or the snow on the mountain. But it's only as you start to put all the pieces together and the whole picture takes shape that you can really see what the little pieces mean.

Genealogy is like a big jigsaw puzzle with a lot of the pieces missing. Tracing your family tree can help you put together a whole picture of your ancestors, your history, and your family's history. It's not always easy; sometimes too many of the pieces are missing. But, just like when you work on a jigsaw puzzle, you find yourself looking for one more piece that will put the whole picture together.

Genealogy is a way of finding out about the people who came before us. It is the stories of the lives of real people who lived in real places in earlier times. Genealogy is part history because our ancestors (the people we are descended from) lived a part of history. They fought in wars, were pioneers, or came over to America as Pilgrims. Or maybe they were Irish immigrants who fled the potato famine. Or perhaps your family emigrated only recently. Genealogy is mostly biography—the story of a person's life. It is also part detective story because we have to find clues about the people who lived so long ago. But most of all, genealogy is fun!

A Collection of Stories

One way to think of genealogy is as a collection of stories. Each person on your family tree is a story waiting to be told. No matter what that person did in his life, he has a story to tell. This book will help you discover how to find those stories. Some of the stories will be dull, but most of them are really interesting. You may be surprised to find out all the great things your ancestors did in their lifetimes. Some of the stories are also a lot of fun. One example is a story of a relative of my husband. This man has been dead for over ninety years but one of his stories is remembered to this day. As a kid, he was famous for his Halloween pranks.

One Halloween he and some friends managed to coax the neighbor's cow up onto the roof of a barn. It took the townspeople most of the next day to get the poor cow back down!

When I go into a school to give a guest talk about genealogy, I start by writing HISTORY on the chalkboard. Then I cross out the HI to show that history is made up of stories. There is one special story I like to tell that shows the difference between history stories and genealogy stories.

On May 15, 1864, in New Market, Virginia, there was a small Civil War battle. It wasn't a very important battle—you probably won't even find it mentioned in your social studies textbook. But it was different from other Civil War battles in one way. The Union troops were trying to sneak down the Shenandoah Valley to cut off Richmond (the Confederate capital) from the rest of the South. They had tried this several times and had always been stopped. This time, the Confederate General Breckinridge knew he needed more men and had to get them fast. So on his way up the valley, he stopped in Lexington, Virginia at the Virginia Military Institute (a preparatory school for boys) and recruited a group of VMI cadets to use as reserve troops. These were just boys, some as young as twelve years old. When the Union and Confederate armies clashed at New Market, Breckinridge's troops were getting beaten. Right at the center of the lines, a gap opened up where his men were being slaughtered. The line started to collapse. Breckinridge had no more troops to send in except the VMI cadets, so he finally gave them the order to attack. The cadets fought bravely and turned the tide of the battle to the Confederate side, stopping the Union advance. VMI is still a military school today. Every year on May 15th, the anniversary of the battle, the roll of the 258 cadets who served in that battle is called. Ten of those cadets were "dead on the field of honor." This story (which I researched and used when I wrote *Cadets at War: The True Story of Teenage Heroism at the Battle of New Market*) is part of our history. It is the story of real people fighting a battle at a real place at a real time, and of some of those people dying in that battle. If your great-grandfather was one of those VMI cadets and saw his friends die on that field, or if your great-grandfather was a Union soldier who watched those boys march forward and fight, then that story is also part of your genealogy— your own stories of your ancestors.

I want to share just a few of the stories I have found in researching my genealogy, just to get you interested in finding your own. Many years ago I was reading the legend of Casey Jones, the train engineer, to some of my third-grade students. One of the children told me he didn't like the story because no engineer would give his life just to stop the train so the passengers wouldn't be killed. The next week I brought in a copy of an old newspaper article about Daniel Lyons, my husband's great-grandfather, who lost his life in a similar accident.

Daniel Lyons was born in County Cork, Ireland, on February 12, 1855, one of nine children of shoemaker Robert Lyne and Joanna Healy. Everyone in Ireland was very poor, and the Lyne children wanted to come to America to make their fortunes. The oldest boy, John, stayed in Ireland with his parents to help his father run the cobbler shop. The others took a ship to America. When they got there, three of the brothers—Robert, Patrick, and Daniel—went to work laying railroad track. They worked hard and eventually all three became railroad engineers. They lived in Springfield, Missouri. Daniel bought land and built houses on it, and made all of his own furniture for his family. But his real love was music, and he spent hours playing his violin. His daughter, Josephine, then fourteen, played the piano very well and planned to become a concert pianist. Daniel had found America to be a great place to live. One night when Daniel was driving his train, he noticed the front wheel on one side seemed loose. He told the station manager about it and asked that it be fixed right away because he thought it might come off. The next night he asked if it had been fixed and was told it had, so he took out his train. He was near the small town of Weaubleau, Missouri, when the wheel came off. He had two choices: to jump and try to save himself or stay with the train to slow it down with the hand brakes. He decided to stay with the train. Only two people died in the train wreck that night: Daniel Lyons and Henry C. Fox, the fireman on the train.

Not all the stories are sad, of course. I always bring to my first class a baby's christening dress. It's not the prettiest christening gown ever made, and some of the sewing isn't very well done. But it was made by a woman for her baby over a hundred years ago. This dress (along with the story after this one) is the thing that really got me started on genealogy so many years ago. The woman who made the dress was a member of the Mohawk tribe living in a one-room cabin in the Canadian backwoods. She supposedly did all the stitching on the dress by firelight. That one-room home seemed great to her—she had grown up living in a longhouse with other members of the tribe. The dress had been passed down through the women of the

family and eventually came to my father's sister for her daughter to wear. Because her daughter had no daughters, the dress then came to my daughter for her christening. When I first held that dress, I knew I had to find out more about this woman's story. As we will later see (Chapter 10), lots of what I heard about the christening dress was not quite true, but that is also a fascinating story in itself.

The second story that started me on genealogy was from my husband's family—a great adventure story about a man who hid in a coffin so the Confederate soldiers wouldn't kill him during the Civil War. James Wilson Beller lived in Charles Town, Virginia (now West Virginia), before the Civil War. In 1844 he started his own newspaper, the *Spirit of Jefferson*, which is still published today. He actually was a strong Confederate supporter, so he probably hid in a coffin to avoid being killed by Union, not Confederate, troops. I don't know if the coffin-hiding story is true, but when the *Spirit of Jefferson* published a special issue on September 20, 1957, to celebrate the fact that Jefferson County, West Virginia, was 150 years old, they wrote about "a vindictive raid by Northern troops" during the Civil War. Their printing presses were damaged in the raid, and they could not publish the paper for six months.

Here's one last story, and then I'll tell you how to start looking for your own stories. This story involves the only ancestor I have whose name really is in the history books—one Martin Prévost who came to Quebec over 300 years ago. In 1644 he married Marie-Olivier Silvestre Manitouabewich, a Huron native woman. Marie's father, a scout for the French trappers, worked with—and became friends with—a fur trader named Olivier LeTardif.

When Marie was ten years old, her father asked his French friend to adopt her so she could be brought up as a French girl. From then on, she lived with the French people. Martin and Marie's marriage was the first marriage recorded in what is now Canada between a Frenchman and a Native American woman.

Finding Your Own Stories

Every family has its own stories. You may find someone very famous among your ancestors, or all your stories may be about regular, everyday people. You will find people who have done very good things in their lives. You may also find people who have done very bad things. The idea behind finding your ancestors is not to find someone famous. The important thing is to find all those everyday people who made up your past.

I once had a client (a person who pays me to find information about his or her family) who wanted very much to believe that he was descended from George Washington and asked me to prove it. I had to tell him that George Washington did not have any children. The two children he raised were his wife's children from her first marriage. This man was very angry with me because I could not prove his relationship.

What that man forgot, and what you must not forget, is that every single person who has ever lived has been an important part of history. Maybe he or she wasn't important to the whole world, but every person is important to his family and to the people who come after him. So don't worry if the people you find in your past are not famous or rich or kings. Without them, you would not even be here! And

that makes them important for you and your research.

Genealogy as History

One thing is important to remember when you are doing genealogical research. Genealogy is history—a story of real people who lived in real places at real times in history. All good genealogists try to do their research carefully without making mistakes. We all do make some, but we TRY to make as few as possible. There are two reasons for this. The first is that, because genealogy is history, you want other people to know that your work is true. That way they will not have to redo everything you do. That's also why it's so important to write down very carefully every piece of information you find and where you found it.

The second reason for not making mistakes is that genealogical research builds on what you have already done. So if you make a mistake and write down the wrong person for your great-grandfather, when you finally realize you've made a mistake, all the work done since will be useless. That can be very frustrating.

How this Book Works

When you do genealogical research, you start out with the things you know. When you run out of information from your own family, you go to your parents' families. You just keep moving further and further back in time.

In the next chapter we will start with information about you and your immediate family. Then we will add your parents' families and learn how to ask the right questions. Only when we've spent a long time on the answers you can find at home or from relatives do we move on to official records.

With official records we start with local records for births, marriages, and deaths, and then talk about land and will records. Then we discuss state records, and finally we talk about national records such as census and military records.

When we run out of official records, we talk about all the other places you can go to find information—libraries and historical societies, cemeteries, church records, and old newspapers. We talk about researching on the Internet for local records, then searching in national and international databases for information.

Genealogy is lots of fun, but there are some things you need to know before you get started. It's important that you not try to understand it all at once, but take it one step at a time. And when we've finished, you'll be surprised at how much you will know.

Getting Started

By now you are ready to start finding your own stories of the past. Before you begin the next chapter, you need the following information:

1. Your full name
2. Your birth date and exact place of birth
3. Your brother(s) and sister(s) full names
4. Your brother(s) and sister(s) birth dates and places of birth
5. Your parents' full names
6. Your parents' dates and places of birth, and date and place of marriage

One good way to get this information is to ask your parents for their marriage record and the birth certificates of everybody in the family.

You and Your Family

With this chapter you begin looking for your own stories of the real people in your past. We need to start by learning about some of the information you should find out about people. We also need to find out the meanings of some of the words you will be using and a way to write down the information so you will be able to find it easily and not lose any of it. The next two chapters cover all these details of genealogy.

What Information Do You Need?

Genealogists start their work with three pieces of information for each of their ancestors: the date and place of birth, marriage, and death. These three facts are the ones that mark the most important events in most people's lives. The records containing these facts are called vital records. Later in this chapter we will look at what these records include. Then, in Chapters 6 and 7, we will discuss how to find and use vital records that you do not have copies of in your family.

We will always be looking for births, marriages, and deaths. But there is other information that we usually look for to make our records complete, such as the name of the church the person attended, his occupation, and any military service. We also write down if they were married at any other time. It is not unusual to have people with two to three other marriages listed. Usually the one you list on your family group sheet is the set of parents, grandparents, etc., from whom you are descended. The others you can list on the back of your form. We will be talking about how to put your information onto family group sheets soon. But first, let's define some genealogical terms.

Definitions

Paternal. Your father's family line; your paternal grandfather is your father's father.

Maternal. Your mother's family line; your maternal grandfather is your mother's father.

Spouse. Husband or wife.

Family Group Sheet. A record that has one whole family on it with all the information for that father and mother and their children in one place.

Vital Records. A record of birth, marriage, or death.

Pedigree Chart. A chart showing all of your direct ancestors—parents, grandparents, great-grandparents, etc. See Chapter 3 for a detailed explanation.

Generation. Each full family group is one generation. You count as the first generation, so a five-generation pedigree chart has you, then your parents as second generation, your grandparents as third generation, your great-grandparents as fourth generation, and your great-great-grandparents as fifth generation.

Occupation. A person's career or work in life.

Document. An official certificate or other written information saying that something is true under law. A birth, marriage, or death certificate is a document. To document something means to show from which official source you took your information.

Deed. A record of the transfer of a piece of real property (land or house) from one person to another. See Chapter 6 for more information.

Will or Probate Records. Records used to distribute everything that a person owns at his death. See Chapter 6 for more information.

Abstract. A short form of a deed or will record that keeps only the important genealogical information.

Family Group Sheets

Many different companies print family group sheets that you can buy. But most of them are complicated and hard to use for someone just starting out doing a family tree. So I have included a simple one at the end of this book that you can use to get started. You can make copies of this, or you can just copy down the informa-tion you will need for each family group using your computer. You can also go to **www.rootsweb.com**, and click on "Blank Charts and Forms" under "Other Tools and Resources" and get forms you can fill in on your computer. There are also free forms at other sites, such as **www.familysearch.org**.

A family group sheet is where you list all the information you can find about one family. I usually keep my stories or pictures of that same family on pages right after the family group sheet. Some people just scan in pictures and documents and keep everything on the computer. On the group sheet you put those three pieces of information (birth, marriage, and death) about each person. All the information here is the kind you get from public records kept by local and state governments. You should always write down where you found the information so you can go back and look at it again if you have to.

Parts of the Family Group Sheet

Look at the sample family group sheet. (There is a blank form you can use on page 93.) Notice the kinds of important information to include:

1. Husband's full name; dates and places of birth, marriage, and death; occupation; military service; church membership; any other marriages; and his parents' names.

2. Wife's full maiden name (the name she had before she got married); dates and places of birth and death; occupation; church membership; any other marriages; and her parents' names.

3. Each child's name; dates and places of birth, marriage, and death; name of spouse(s).

4. A place to list sources of information for the husband and wife. Sources on children can be listed with this information.

Family Group Sheet Number: _16_

Husband: _BELLER, Ephraim S._

	Date	Place	Source
Birth:			
Marriage:	30 May 1816	Jefferson Cty, W. Va.	m. cert.
Death:			
Occupation:	Cabinetmaker	Military Service: War of 1812	
Church:	Methodist	Other Marriages: no	
Father:	Peter Beller	Mother: Amelia Sagathy	

Wife: _REED, Sarah_

	Date	Place	Source
Birth:	1793	Charlestown, Jeff Cty, W. Va.	Census
Marriage:	30 May 1816	Jefferson Cty, W. Va.	m. cert.
Death:	14 May 1870	Charlestown, Jeff Cty, W. Va.	d. cert.
Occupation:	Homemaker		
Church:	Methodist	Other Marriages:	
Father:		Mother:	

Children (Start with oldest):

Name	Birth	Marriage	Spouse	Death
James Wilson	1 Jun 1819 West Virginia	17 Feb 1848 Charlestown no m. cert. — newspaper notice	Jane Elizabeth Kelly	22 Oct 1877 Charlestown no d. cert.; obituary bur: Edge Hill Cem.
Amelia R.	1823	none	none	1 Jan 1875 Charlestown, W. Va. d. cert.: age 52, pneumonia
John M.	1827	none	none	20 Jan 1873 Charlestown, W. Va. d. cert.: age 46, printer
Charles Edward	Dec 1834 Charlestown, W. Va.	2 Apr 1857 Winchester, VA m. cert.	Ella Virginia Haines	9 Mar 1909 Washington, DC d. cert. bur: Edge Hill Cem.

Documenting

If you use a birth, marriage, or death certificate, write down b. cert., m. cert., or d. cert. in the source column. Include the volume and page number if there is one.

If you find your information in a family Bible, write BIBLE. Then, on the back of the sheet, write FAMILY BIBLE, currently owned by [name and address]. If you use a family Bible, it's a good idea to photocopy all of the listings since you might not get to see it often.

If you find your information in a census or military record, include all the information on the back of your sheet or on a separate piece of paper.

If you find your information in a book, write down all the information about the book so you can find it again if you need to. Include the library or collection you saw it in, along with the other bibliographic data: title, author, publisher, and copyright date.

If you find your information on a website, be sure to write down its URL. Also write down where the information on the website came from.

Birth Certificate

Look at the sample birth certificate on the next page. This is a copy of an official standard certificate. Old birth records sometimes gave very little information. These new ones are more complete. Most states now use one like this. Let's look at some of the information you can learn from this.

Child:
Name (some will just say "baby boy" or "baby girl" if the parents did not select a name before the record was filed)
Date and time of birth
Place of birth

Mother:
Full maiden name
Age
Her place of birth (state or country)

Father:
Full name
Age
His place of birth (state or country)

The rest of the information is used by the state health department and does not appear in the records you get at the vital records office.

Marriage Certificate

Look at the sample marriage certificate on page 22. This is a copy of an official standard marriage certificate. Very old marriage records usually gave only the names of the bride and groom and the date of their marriage. Later on, the names of their parents were included in marriage records. That really helped because it let researchers add another whole family to their pedigree chart.

The information given today can really help in your research. Here is a list of some of the important information.

Groom:
Full name
Where he lives
State and date of birth—with these two pieces of information you can try to get his birth certificate
Father's name and state of birth
Mother's maiden name and state of birth

Bride:
Full name and maiden name (if different)—this might give you a clue whether she was married before
Where she lives
State and date of birth

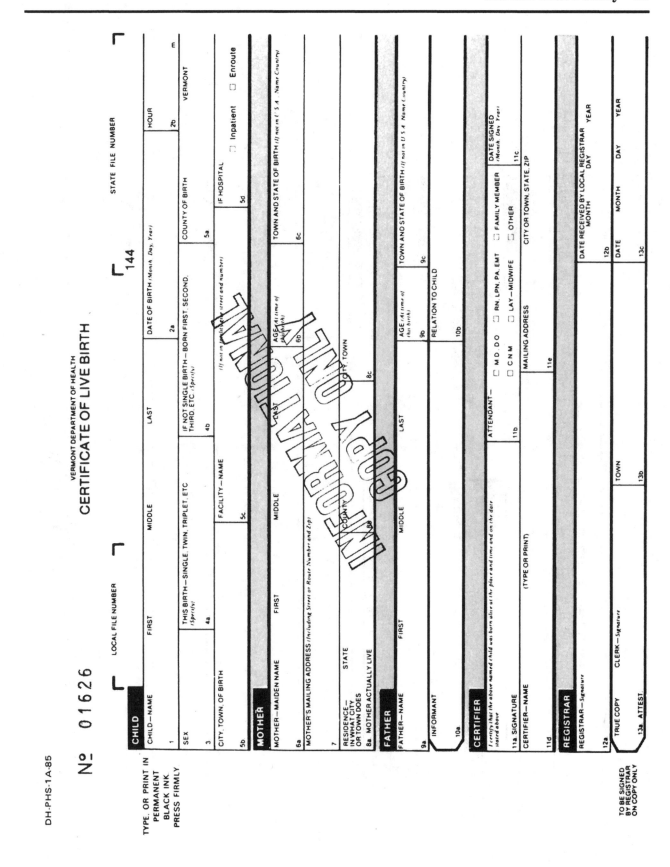

DH-PHS-1A-85

Nº 01626

VERMONT DEPARTMENT OF HEALTH
CERTIFICATE OF LIVE BIRTH

TYPE, OR PRINT IN PERMANENT BLACK INK PRESS FIRMLY

STATE FILE NUMBER

LOCAL FILE NUMBER

144

CHILD

CHILD—NAME | FIRST | MIDDLE | LAST | DATE OF BIRTH (Month, Day, Year) | HOUR
1 | | | | 2a | 2b m

SEX | THIS BIRTH—SINGLE, TWIN, TRIPLET, ETC (Specify) | IF NOT SINGLE BIRTH—BORN FIRST, SECOND, THIRD, ETC (Specify) | COUNTY OF BIRTH | VERMONT
3 | 4a | 4b | 5a

CITY, TOWN, OF BIRTH | FACILITY—NAME | IF HOSPITAL — Inpatient — Enroute
5b | 5c | 5d

MOTHER

MOTHER—MAIDEN NAME | FIRST | MIDDLE | LAST | AGE (At time of this birth) | TOWN AND STATE OF BIRTH (If not in U.S.A. Name Country)
6a | | | | 6b | 6c

MOTHER'S MAILING ADDRESS (Including Street or Route Number and Zip)
7

RESIDENCE— IN WHAT CITY OR TOWN DOES | STATE | COUNTY | CITY, TOWN
8a MOTHER ACTUALLY LIVE | 8b | 8c

FATHER

FATHER—NAME | FIRST | MIDDLE | LAST | AGE (At time of this birth) | TOWN AND STATE OF BIRTH (If not in U.S.A. Name Country)
9a | | | | 9b | 9c

INFORMANT | RELATION TO CHILD
10a | 10b

CERTIFIER

I certify that the above named child was born alive at the place and time and on the date stated above | ATTENDANT— — MD, DO — RN, LPN, PA, EMT — FAMILY MEMBER — CNM — LAY—MIDWIFE — OTHER | DATE SIGNED (Month Day Year)
11a SIGNATURE | 11b | 11c

CERTIFIER—NAME (TYPE OR PRINT) | MAILING ADDRESS | CITY OR TOWN, STATE, ZIP
11d | 11e

REGISTRAR

REGISTRAR—Signature | DATE RECEIVED BY LOCAL REGISTRAR MONTH   DAY   YEAR
12a | 12b

TO BE SIGNED BY REGISTRAR ON COPY ONLY

TRUE COPY | CLERK—Signature | TOWN | DATE   MONTH   DAY   YEAR
13a ATTEST | 13b | 13c

INFORMATIONAL COPY ONLY

OH-PHS-9-83

41059

TYPE OR PRINT IN PERMANENT BLACK INK PRESS FIRMLY

LOCAL FILE NUMBER

STATE FILE NUMBER

VERMONT DEPARTMENT OF HEALTH

CERTIFICATE OF MARRIAGE

(DECLARATION OF INTENTION AND MARRIAGE CERTIFICATE)

INFORMATIONAL COPY ONLY

1 GROOM

| NAME | 1 | FIRST | MIDDLE | LAST |

MAILING ADDRESS | STREET OR R.F.D. | CITY/TOWN | STATE | ZIP

2

3A. RESIDENCE – IN WHAT CITY OR TOWN DOES GROOM ACTUALLY LIVE | STATE 3B | COUNTY 3C

4A. DATE OF BIRTH (Month, Day, Year) | 4B. STATE OF BIRTH (If not in U.S.A. Name Country) | 4C. FATHER–Full Name | 4D. MOTHER–Full Maiden Name

BRIDE

| NAME | 5 | FIRST | MIDDLE | LAST |

MAILING ADDRESS | 7A | STREET OR R.F.D. | CITY/TOWN | STATE | ZIP

6

8. RESIDENCE – IN WHAT CITY OR TOWN DOES BRIDE ACTUALLY LIVE | STATE 7B | COUNTY 7C

9A. DATE OF BIRTH (Month, Day, Year) | 9B. STATE OF BIRTH (If not in U.S.A. Name Country) | 9C. FATHER–Full Name | 9D. MOTHER–Full Maiden Name

10A. DATE OF BIRTH (Month, Day, Year) | 10B. STATE OF BIRTH (If not in U.S.A. Name Country) | 12A. STATE OF BIRTH (If not in U.S.A. Name Country) | 12B. MAIDEN NAME–(If different)

APPLICANT

WE HEREBY CERTIFY THAT THE INFORMATION PROVIDED IS CORRECT TO THE BEST OF OUR KNOWLEDGE AND BELIEF AND THAT WE ARE FREE TO MARRY UNDER THE LAWS OF VERMONT.

| 13A APPLICANT–Signature | 13B DATE SIGNED | 13C APPLICANT–Signature | 13D DATE SIGNED |

CERTIFICATION

I hereby certify that the above named persons have made oath to the truth of the facts stated in the foregoing declaration of intention of marriage and complied with the marriage laws of the State of Vermont. A medical certificate or waiver, as per 18 V.S.A. 5136-5137, is on file in this office.

| 14A DATE ON WHICH LICENSE WAS ISSUED | 14B TOWN OR CITY | 14C |
| 14D THIS LICENSE IS VALID FROM _____ DATE _____ TO _____ DATE _____ UNLESS WAIVED BY A VERMONT COURT. |

TOWN CLERK–Signature

OFFICIANT

This license authorizes the marriage of the above named couple by any person duly authorized to perform a marriage ceremony. THIS LICENSE IS VALID ONLY IN VERMONT.

I CERTIFY THAT THE ABOVE PERSONS WERE MARRIED ON THIS DATE:

| 15A OFFICIANT–Signature | 15B DATE SIGNED (Month, Day, Year) | 15C CITY/TOWN AND COUNTY OF MARRIAGE: | 15D |
| 15E RELIGIOUS OR CIVIL OFFICIAL (Specify) |

TO BE SIGNED BY REGISTRAR ON COPY ONLY

CLERK'S SIGNATURE

TRUE COPY–Clerk Signature

16A OFFICIANT–Signature | 16B TOWN | 16C DATE RECEIVED BY LOCAL REGISTRAR

17A Attest: | 17B TOWN | 17C DATE

Father's name and state of birth
Mother's maiden name and state of
   birth

You can see that if you don't know any-thing else about this couple, you can find a lot of useful information on the marriage certificate. You would have their parents' names and places of birth, so you could start looking for their birth certificates. This one record could give you many ideas of places to go for more information.

Death Certificate

Look at the sample death certificate on page 24. This is the standard official death record used in most states today. Early death records gave almost as much information. Usually they contained the person's name, date of death, cause of death, the person's age, name of husband or wife, and occupation. Today the records also ask for the names of the person's parents (but no state of birth for them) and include the person's date of birth and the state where he or she was born. With that information you might try to get a birth record. Much of the information on this form will not help you. What would be helpful is

to write down the place of burial since that would lead you to cemetery records, which possibly contain more information.

Homework

Before we go on to Chapter 3, you need to actually do the work we've talked about in Chapter 2. Make a family group sheet for your immediate family like the sample one in this chapter. Fill in all of the information you can. Be sure to use full names and document your information from actual records if you can.

For the next chapter you will need to get the same types of information for your parents' families:

- The full names of your grandparents
- Your grandparents' dates and plac-es of birth, marriage, and death (if necessary)
- The full names of your grandparents' children (your aunts and uncles)
- The children's dates and places of birth, marriage, and death (if necessary)
- The names of the children's spouses

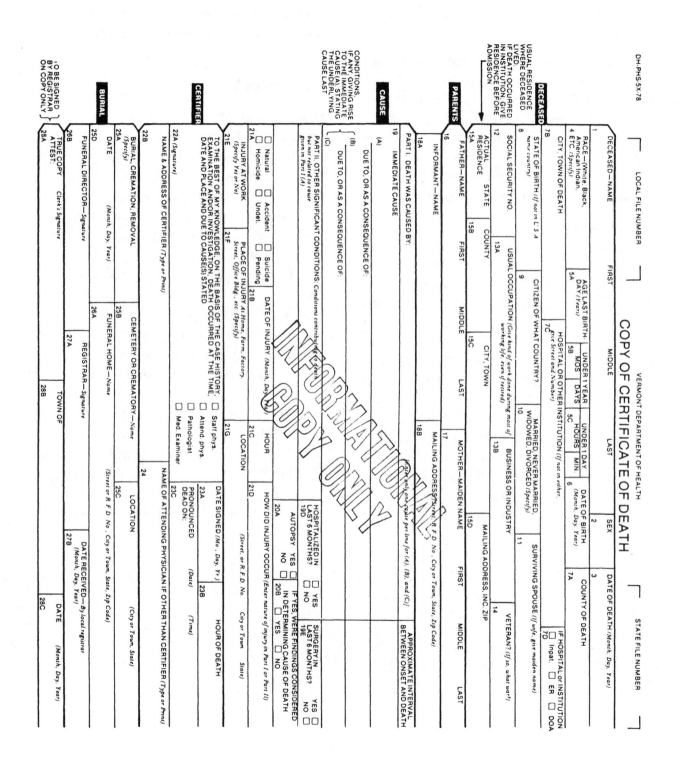

Your Parents' Families

As we begin Chapter 3, you will have filled in one family group sheet. By the end of this chapter, you will have filled in two more group sheets and will have started a pedigree chart.

There are some little things you can do to make all of your family group sheets look the same and help you find information more quickly. These are:

1. Always put the family last name first and in capital letters for both the husband's and wife's names. Example: BELLER, Walter Michael. This really helps if you get a confusing name later on and can't remember which is first or last.

2. Always write out the full name if you know it, including the middle name.

3. For women, always use the full maiden name. That way each group sheet always shows two family lines—the husband with his parents and the wife with hers.

4. When you start doing genealogical research, you will find that most genealogists put the day before the month when they are writing a date. It is very important to pick one system and use the same system all the time. Otherwise, when you see 6/5/1857 you won't know whether it is

May 6, 1857, or June 5, 1857. Notice also that I wrote out 1857. Always write out the year, because once you get going you'll be using 1600s, 1700s, 1800s, and 1900s, and you'll need to keep them straight. I use a simpler date system that prevents mix-ups. Put the day first but use a three-letter abbreviation for the month instead of using another number. So I would write 6 May 1857 or 5 Jun 1857. The abbreviations for the months are:

Jan	– January	Jul	– July
Feb	– February	Aug	– August
Mar	– March	Sep	– September
Apr	– April	Oct	– October
May	– May	Nov	– November
Jun	– June	Dec	– December

With this new information it's time to redo your first family group sheet using these rules. As you copy it over, check also that you have always written down your sources of information. You can look back at Chapter 2 at the filled-in family group sheet to make sure you have done everything correctly. At the top of your family group sheet where it says "Number," write down "2." I will explain why when we get to the pedigree chart.

Now it is time to take all of the information you have gotten on your parents' families and fill in two new group sheets: one with your father's father as head of the family (Family Group #4), and one with your mother's father as head of the family (Family Group #6).

As you start to fill in these two sheets, you will probably get to the point where you do not have actual birth records to use. You might have a family Bible if you are lucky. You will want to fill in these blank spaces by using vital records.

Pedigree Charts

A pedigree chart is a way of listing all of your ancestors on one form. You can see your family tree as it goes back and see the branching. The pedigree chart lets you see at a glance how far you have gone in your research. There are many kinds of pedigree charts. Some are made to look like trees with branches. Some are shaped like fans. The sample pedigree chart I have included is a simple, all-purpose chart to get you started. In the back of the book is a blank copy you can use to make copies for your own research. As your research goes further along, you might need a larger pedigree chart of some kind to keep track of all your lines.

Some pedigree charts just give you room to list the names. Others list data for the first few generations. Pedigree charts are easy to use and they help keep all your family group sheets in order. To make it easier, put last names in capital letters again so you'll always know which is which. I have taken a pedigree chart and filled in the name blanks with relationships (father, mother, grandfather, etc.) so you can see how easy it is. Study this sheet before we go on to discuss how it is numbered, which is the only tricky part to using these charts.

Numbering

If you look at the sample five-generation pedigree chart, you can see that you are number 1, your father is number 2, and your mother is number 3 on the chart. You can see that the male lines all have even numbers (2, 4, 6, 8, 10, 12, 14, 16, 18, 20, 22, 24, 26, 28, 30). The wives of each family group have odd numbers (3, 5, 7, 9, 11, 13, 15, 17, 19, 21, 23, 25, 27, 29, 31). The wife's number is always the number after her husband's number. For example, since your paternal grandfather is #4, your paternal grandmother must be #5.

Now comes the tricky part. Every generation back doubles the number of the person in the generation before. The father of #4 is 4 x 2 or #8. The father of #12 is 12 x 2 or #24. The father of #15 is 15 x 2 or #30. And the neat thing about this system is that it goes on and on. The father of #20 is #40. The father of #40 is #80 and it keeps going. The biggest number on my pedigree chart is in the 30,000s, but it all comes from multiplying each generation by two. If you find it confusing at first, that's okay. It takes some time to get used to. But as you get going, you'll be surprised at how easy it becomes.

Family group sheets are always written with the husband's name first. That's why they all have even numbers. So all your family group sheets will have an even number, and you can just keep them in numerical order. No matter how far back you go, you don't need to change the system. There are some very complicated systems you will see in some books or in printed family histories, but most people try to keep it simple and easy to use.

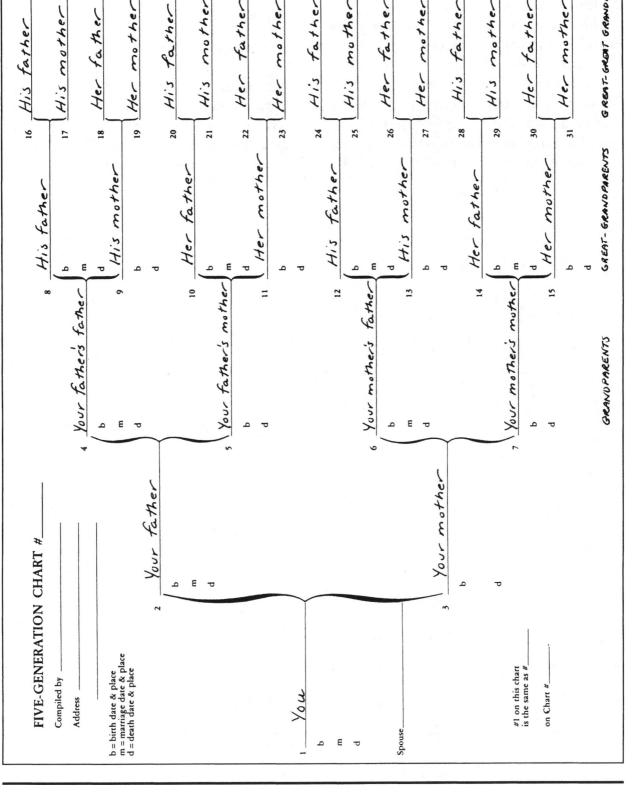

FIVE-GENERATION CHART # _____

Compiled by _____

Address _____

b = birth date & place
m = marriage date & place
d = death date & place

1 You _____
b
m
d

Spouse _____

#1 on this chart
is the same as # _____
on Chart # _____.

2 Your Father _____
b
m
d

3 Your mother _____
b
d

4 Your father's father _____
b
m
d

5 Your father's mother _____
b
d

6 Your mother's father _____
b
m
d

7 Your mother's mother _____
b
d

8 His father _____
b
m
d

9 His mother _____
b
d

10 Her father _____
b
d

11 Her mother _____
b
d

12 His father _____
b
m
d

13 His mother _____
b
d

14 Her father _____
b
m
d

15 Her mother _____
b
d

16 His father _____
17 His mother _____
18 Her father _____
19 Her mother _____
20 His father _____
21 His mother _____
22 Her father _____
23 Her mother _____
24 His father _____
25 His mother _____
26 Her father _____
27 Her mother _____
28 His father _____
29 His mother _____
30 Her father _____
31 Her mother _____

See Chart #

GRANDPARENTS   GREAT-GRANDPARENTS   GREAT-GREAT GRANDPARENTS

Make a copy of the blank sample and put your name on line 1. Then put your father's name on line 2 and your mother's on line 3. Your father's parents go on lines 4 and 5. Your mother's parents go on lines 6 and 7. And just keep going.

One question I am sometimes asked is what you do if you are in a stepfamily. When you are researching, you usually use your own father and mother for lines 2 and 3. But there is no rule that says you can't add your stepfather's or stepmother's lines to your research. Remember, you are doing the research *you* are interested in.

Homework

You should finish copying information on family group sheets 4 and 6 at this time. You can also begin on sheets 8, 10, 12, and 14 just from information your parents can give you. In the next chapter we will discuss interviewing people to fill in answers on those new group sheets.

Asking Questions: Genealogy as Oral History

You've been working on your family tree for some time now. You've looked at all the records your parents have at home. You've seen your birth certificate and those of your parents and brothers and sisters. You've seen your parents' marriage certificate. Your mother and father have given you as much information as they can remember about their parents and their brothers and sisters. You've recorded everything. You now have three family group sheets: 1) one for your own family with your father's name as head (Family Group #2); 2) one for your father's own family with your paternal grandfather's name as head (FG #4); and 3) one for your mother's own family with your maternal grandfather's name as head (FG #6).

So what's next? Now it's time to move out into the world and get some answers. The first step is to talk to other relatives—especially older relatives like grandparents and great-grandparents, great-aunts and great-uncles. These people, who have lived so much longer than your parents, have all sorts of information you need. But how do you begin? In this chapter we'll talk about whom to ask, when to ask

them, and most importantly, what to ask them. We'll also talk about how to ask and whether to take notes or tape-record your conversations with them.

Whom Should I Ask?

You should make a list of older relatives in your parents' families who might be able to answer your questions. Your grandparents are a great place to start. Start with someone you know—you might feel a bit silly asking all these questions at first. It's easier if the person is someone you know well. After you've exhausted the people you know, start with others you don't know as well. Remember that this is supposed to be fun. So if you have an older relative you don't feel comfortable with, don't start with that person.

When Do I Ask?

This is one of those really simple questions. But it is very important. You can't call your grandmother when she's busy making dinner and expect her to be happy to answer all your questions. You may need to set a special time for your interview. You want a time when you will not be disturbed. In the beginning you need to interview one person at a time. You also should not schedule a lengthy interview. Just plan on asking a few questions at first. Your parents can help by talking with relatives for you to help set up an interview. But remember, the research is yours. You shouldn't have your parents do the interviewing for you.

What Should I Ask?

Imagine that you did something that made you instantly famous. If someone came to interview you and said, "Tell me everything about you and your family," you wouldn't know what to answer. The question is too general. The situation is the same when you interview family members. The rule for asking questions is to make the questions simple enough that they can be easily answered.

Let's try to come up with a list of the kinds of questions that might be good to ask. We want questions that will give us our "stories." We want questions that will let people remember some of the special things that happened in their lives. The answers to our questions should tell us what it was like to be a kid when they were growing up. (Remember the Halloween story I told you about earlier.) Finally, the questions should tell us something about the people around the person being interviewed, so we can learn about them too.

When I teach a genealogy class, we "brainstorm" questions so that each person has an emergency list of things to ask if they run out of their own questions. We start out with categories of questions: family, holidays, houses, pets, school,

things (cars, favorite toys, TV, radio), and then put questions for each category. Listed here are some of the questions that I have brainstormed with students in my classes:

Family:
How did you celebrate your birthday?
What kinds of things did the whole family do together—play games, listen to radio, etc.?
Did you have an older brother or sister take care of you? Did you have to take care of a younger brother or sister?
What's the favorite thing you remember about your mother when you were a child?
What's the favorite thing you remember about your father when you were a child?
Do you remember your grandparents? What were they like? Did you see them often?
Were you in the military? Which war, where were you stationed, what did you do?

Holidays:
What was the first thing you used to do on Christmas morning?
How did you decorate your Christmas tree?
What kinds of tricks did you play for Halloween?
What did you dress up as for Halloween?
What did you have for Thanksgiving dinner?
Did you have Thanksgiving dinner at home or at someone else's house? Who was there?
Did you celebrate New Year's Eve? How?

Did you dye Easter eggs? Did you have an Easter egg hunt or roll?

What special goodies did you have at special times of the year?

Did you have a Fourth of July parade? Fireworks?

What church or place of worship did you go to?

Were there special holidays/holy days celebrated as part of your religion? What were they and how were they celebrated?

Pets:

Did you have any pets? What were their names? What kind? What color? What happened to them?

Favorite Things:

What was your favorite toy?

What was your favorite food? What foods did you NOT like?

Did you have a favorite place to go to be alone?

Did you have a place where you and your friends met (a treehouse, the corner drugstore, etc.)?

What was your first car like?

What was the best present you ever received?

Tell me about dances and dates when you were a teenager. Where did you go?

What was your favorite vacation?

Houses:

Did you live in a city or in the country?

What was your house like (how many rooms, floors, etc.)?

Did you have your own bedroom?

What chores did you have to do at home?

Did you have a TV, radio, record player?

School:

What was your school building like?

How many people were in a class?

What was your favorite subject?

What did you like least about school?

Did you ever get in trouble in school?

Did you have a favorite teacher?

Did you go to a town library?

What were your favorite books?

What games did you play at recess?

What was the name of your best friend?

Asking Genealogy Questions

Of course, as much as you are enjoying all these stories, you are also supposed to be finding information for your family group sheets. So, in the middle of other questions, you can ask more specific ones. Don't ever ask only those because people get tired of them quickly. They also sometimes get upset because they can't remember the answers.

Some Questions to Ask:

When was your mother's birthday (month and day)?

When was your father's birthday (month and day)?

What were your brothers' and sisters' names?

When were your brothers' and sisters' birthdays?

Whom did they marry? When (not date— just "when I was about twelve")? Where?

Do you remember your grandmother's and grandfather's names (one person at a time)? Where did he/she live? What time of year was his/her birthday?

Why Some of the Answers Are Wrong

One of the most important things to

remember is that some of the answers will not be right. People forget things. They won't forget the stories but they will forget the names and places and dates. Once I could not find a death record because everyone remembered that the person died in May when he actually died in November.

You need to take the genealogical information you are given and check it with vital records or a family Bible or church records. But you can just copy down the stories to enjoy even if some of them are "tall" tales.

Remember also that the idea of the questions is to start people talking. You may find someone who will go from subject to subject, and you won't have to say much at all. Another person may only answer the exact question you ask.

How to Interview

When you interview people, you can write down notes to remember what they said. But the best thing to do is use a tape recorder. Even better is to record the interview with a movie camera. Some people will not want to talk on a tape recorder or be in a movie, but many won't mind. You may have to start out taking notes. But then you might say, "Grandpa, I know you don't like the tape recorder, but I really would like to have your story about your first car in your own words. Could you tell just that one on tape?" He may say no, but he may say yes.

It is important that the people you are interviewing feel comfortable. I once tape-recorded a very special conversation. My husband's grandmother, who was ninety-five years old, would not talk about the past. She was living in the future and thought the past was boring. One

day I asked her if I could tape her playing the piano, which she still did beautifully. That she would allow. Once she got used to the tape recorder, she started talking about how she learned to play the piano and then about her father. She died when she was ninety-nine years old, and that tape is fantastic to listen to now.

There are three more things I want to say here. The first is to do your questioning soon. There are lots of people I wish I could have taped. Many of their stories are lost forever.

The second thing is that you must remember to respect people's right to privacy. No one HAS to talk to you. If someone says no, that's okay. Don't make her feel bad—she may change her mind later. If someone will answer questions but won't let you tape or take notes, just remember the story as best you can and write it down when you get home. And if someone tells you something and asks that you not tell someone else, it is very important that you always do what he asks. People will not talk to you if you do not respect their right to privacy.

The third and most important point of all—HAVE FUN! It's not important that you find all the answers—or even most of them. Try to find enough that you will have some great things to remember about the person. But keep in mind that you'll also want to remember later how much fun you had talking together. Once that person dies, the memory of that special time will mean even more than all the information you got from them.

Homework

Interview at least one person before going on to the next chapter. Try to find information to fill in family group sheets #8, 10, 12, and 14, and get the names for the fifth generation on their pedigree charts.

In Chapter 5 we will try to put all our research together. This will help us get ready to research on the Internet and beyond.

Putting It All Together

This chapter is the last of the "how-to" chapters for your genealogy. After this chapter, the remainder of this book is about different kinds of materials that can give us genealogical information. We'll also be talking about the places where this information can be found. From now on there is no special homework assigned for each chapter. I will give you some advice for getting organized and continuing your work, and give you examples of ways to put things together. Sometimes I will suggest a homework activity to try to further your research.

What Do You Have?

If you have been following along with the homework assignments so far, you should have a pedigree chart with your own name, your parents' names, your grandparents' names, and hopefully, most of your great-grandparents' names filled in. The numbers on your pedigree chart stop at 31. For each even number beginning with number 2, you have a matching family group

sheet. That means you have fifteen family group sheets numbered 2, 4, 6, 8, 10, 12, 14, 16, 18, 20, 22, 24, 26, 28, and 30. The group sheets are for the families shown in the chart on the following page.

At this point in your research, with a pedigree chart and fifteen family group sheets to work with, it is a good idea to get a looseleaf binder to keep it all in. Put the pedigree chart first and then put in all the family group sheets in numerical order from the lowest to the highest number. Now every time you get information about someone, you can add that information to the correct group sheet. If it is extra information—like a "story" for your collection—you can put it on a piece of looseleaf paper right after the family group sheet that lists that person. For example, when you talked to your maternal grandmother, she told a story about how her parents celebrated her birthday and those of her brothers and sisters. You should write that story on a piece of paper and put it behind group sheet #14 because it is about things that happened in that family.

Generation	FG#	Family	Head of Family
2	2	Your own family	Your father
3	4	Your father's family	Your father's father
	6	Your mother's family	Your mother's father
4	8		
	10		
	12	Your 4 grandparents' families	Your great-grandparents
	14		
5	16		
	18		
	20		
	22		
	24	Your 8 great-grandparents' families	Your great-great-grandparents
	26		
	28		
	30		

What Do You Need?

Take the time now to put all your sheets in order as described above. Once you have done that, it is time to look at all the sheets and determine what information is missing. Start with FG #2 and go through it line by line, checking the information you have. Below is a list of questions to ask yourself as you check each one. Once you have been doing genealogical research for a while, you won't need a checklist like this. You will be able to tell what is missing just by glancing at your sheet. But for now, it is important to notice every part. So, with group sheet #2 in front of you, start answering these questions. Every time your answer to a question is "no," make a note to yourself of what is missing.

Remember that you do not need to do all this right now. My students do this over the course of two or three weeks. If you try to do it all at once, you'll probably get discouraged. It's better to take your time.

What to Do Next?

Now that you have checked over all of your family group sheets, it's time to decide where to go for your missing information. Notice that on the sample form I put a column for "What to do now." I have filled in some suggestions for your sample page. Since each situation is different, it's hard to tell you where you should look next without seeing your actual information, but here are a few general rules to follow.

1. Try home sources first.
2. Always try to find vital records (births, marriages, and deaths) next; they are the easiest to track down.

3. If you are trying to put an old family group together, think of vital records (Chapter 6), will records (Chapter 6), or census records (Chapter 8).

4. Once you know where a family lived, using land records can help you find out when and where they came there and/or when they left and where they went (Chapter 6). State and national censuses can help with this too.

5. If the husband was in his late teens or twenties during wartime, check the military records—maybe you'll find him there (Chapter 8).

One important thing to keep in mind is that what you are learning to do in this chapter does not change, no matter how long you are involved in doing genealogical research. You will be constantly adding new information, putting it in place, and deciding what to look for next. As you do this, you will gradually move further and further back in your lines of ancestors.

Remember also what I said in the beginning of Chapter 1. There are some answers you will never find, because the records you need to provide the information just don't exist anymore. You are putting the jigsaw puzzle of your ancestors together with only the pieces you happen to find. That's why genealogy can be very frustrating at times! But the fun comes in always searching, and in finding a piece of material you thought you'd never see.

Checklist		
For husband do I have:	**For wife do I have:**	**For each child do I have:**
□ Full name	□ Full maiden name	□ Full name
□ Birth date, place, and source	□ Birth date, place, and source	□ Birth date, place, and source
□ Marriage date, place, and source	□ Death date, place, and source	□ Marriage date, place, and source
□ Death date, place, and source	□ Occupation	□ Name of spouse
□ Occupation	□ Church attended	□ Death date, place, and source
□ Military service information	□ Other marriages	
□ Church attended	□ Father's name	
□ Other marriages	□ Mother's name	
□ Father's name		
□ Mother's name		

Certificate of Marriage

GROOM
NAME:
ADDRESS:
DATE OF BIRTH:
STATE OF BIRTH:

BRIDE
NAME:
ADDRESS:
DATE OF BIRTH:
STATE OF BIRTH:

Kinds of Records Found Locally

In Chapters 1–5 we talked about using records that are available within your own family. We looked at the information given on a birth, marriage, or death record, and saw samples of them. Now that you have used up all of your family sources, it's time to talk about genealogical research outside of family information. For the rest of this book, we will discuss some of the major kinds of official records containing genealogical information.

We will also talk about other sources of information: local histories, church records, and old newspapers. You will not be able to use some of the records I will discuss, since only adults are allowed to visit some of the libraries or other places where genealogical information is located. You will find, however, that you can access many of the records on the Internet. We will talk about some good online places to start looking for them.

We start out this chapter with the simplest of the genealogical information available outside the family—vital records. We will also talk about other records that are found locally, such as deeds, wills, and local court records. These records are kept right in the communities where they occurred—the towns, cities, or counties themselves. Copies of these records are also usually kept at some state offices.

Where Vital Records Are Kept

Vital records are the most important records for doing genealogical research. Unfortunately, for many years vital records were not kept. Births and deaths were not recorded regularly until after the Civil War and in many states not until after 1900. In many of the cases where they were kept, they have not survived. Many records were destroyed in fires. Other records may have been destroyed by war, especially in Virginia counties during the Civil War. Many records have been destroyed by neglect. Some were written down on cheap paper that has fallen to pieces. Some clerks used ink that has faded so much that it cannot be read at all. I know of at least one county, and many people have told me of others, where old records are sitting in attics and being eaten up by rats. Because these are local records, with each individual jurisdiction (a jurisdiction is an area controlled by an official government, so you might have a town or a county or a state government) making its own decisions on how to care for its records, you will find great differences from place to place in the condition of the records. Some areas have complete records in perfect condition. In others you will find very little information.

In some states a copy has been made of every single vital record found in the smaller jurisdictions like towns or cities, and all the copies are available in one place. Vermont is one such state, and you can research all of Vermont's old vital records on microfilm in one place. Members of The Church of Jesus Christ of Latter-day Saints (LDS Church) have tried to get permission to put all old local records on microfilm. This includes vital records, as well as land, will, and court records. Most communities have allowed their records to be copied so that researchers can use them at any of the LDS genealogical libraries (Family History Centers) around the country. Other communities will not allow their records to be filmed.

Another point to keep in mind with these records is that they are not always accurate. I once found two different birth records for an ancestor I was researching. Neither of them matched the birth date on his death record, which was the one his family said was right. Mistakes can be caused by a clerk taking down the information incorrectly—names especially can be a mess. Sometimes families registered all of their children's births at once, years after they were born. You must keep in mind that there are all sorts of weird surprises in the official records.

I am taking the time to show you the problems with vital records to make a point. The availability of vital records is very different from place to place. It is important that you find out what the situation is at your location before trying to do research. You don't want to find that the records are not there and feel that you've wasted your time. It is also important to know that many of the places will not want students doing research, and if you don't seem to know what you're doing, they will not give you any chance at all. In the next chapter we will talk about how you can find these records and use them in your family history.

You may be working with vital records in person or on the Internet. Often what you will use are indexes that have been made of the vital records. Many of the local clerks' offices have had their records indexed. This is a favorite project for local genealogical or historical societies. Some places still have no indexes to their records but that is changing quickly.

If you are lucky enough to be using the actual record books themselves, you will find an old kind of system for indexing them. An index, or list of names of the people in the records, is very useful. Without one, researchers would have to read every line in the book unless they happened to already know the exact date of the birth, marriage, or death they were looking for. In the front of the books where the births and deaths are recorded (many places have these two together in one book), there is a set of pages with alphabet tabs along the edges. When the clerk records a birth, he or she turns to the correct letter of the alphabet for the person's last name and lists the name there along with the page on which the record can be found. So this is an index by first letter of last name only. In a thick vital records volume you might have to read through several hundred last names beginning with B to find the one you want. The book may also have two indexes if it has both birth and death records—one index for births and one for deaths.

The second kind of old index is like the first except that it breaks the letters down further, so there might be pages for BA, BE, BI, BL, BR, and BU. Be careful with this kind because the spelling of the clerks was not always accurate. I have found Beller spelled as Bellar, Baller, Ballar, Biller, Billew, and others. So with that kind of index, you still need to look at all the Bs. After a while you get really good at picking out your name on a page of names—even with the old-fashioned handwriting.

The lesson here is always to look through the book before you begin using it so that you understand its system and don't miss any information.

Getting Vital Records

It is quite possible that you will need to either write to get vital records or fill in some information to order them online. Especially after your research starts to go far back, you will probably find that well over half of the people you are looking for did not live anywhere near where you live.

Let's say that you have a name and a date of birth. You decide to write to the county or town clerk to get the record. You must remember that these clerks are often very busy people. If they get a letter asking for "everything you have on William Smith," they will send it back and say that they do not do genealogical research. You'll get the same kind of answer if you send a list of fifteen records and ask for copies of all of them. But if you send the fee along with a nice clear letter ask-

ing for only two records and giving lots of information that will help their search, you will usually get an answer.

The most important part about finding the record you want—whether in person, by letter, or on the Internet—is to give enough information to find the person. Let's look at the kind of information you'd want to give to get each of the three kinds of vital records.

Birth:
   Full name
   Date of birth
   Place of birth
   Names of parents

Marriage:
   Full names of both bride and groom
   Date and place of marriage
   Names of their parents (if you know them)

Death:
   Full name
   Date and place of birth
   Date and place of death
   Names of parents and/or spouse

I realize that as you look at the list, your first thought is that if you knew all that stuff, you wouldn't need the record at all. But this is just here to get you started. Obviously, you won't know most of this, but it will help you provide as much information as possible so that you stand a better chance of getting your answer.

Land, Will, and Court Records

The other records that are kept at the local level are not as easy to use as vital records, and they do not give as much information. But when the vital records are not available, either because the time period you are looking for is before the records were kept or because the records no longer exist, these can be a great help. I will explain how each type of record is kept, what information it contains, and how to use it. These are all complicated legal records, and my explanation only tells a few things about them. I am just giving you an idea of when you might want to use them and what you will find if you do.

Land Records

There are two kinds of land records. One is the kind that gave the land to the first person ever to own it when a state or territory was first settled. This type of record is called a land grant or a patent. These records go back to the beginnings of the colonies and then the states, when all the land was still owned by the state or national government. These records may be kept at the local level or may be found in a state office.

The other kind of land record is used when one owner gives the ownership of the land to another person. This is called a deed record and is kept in the town or county clerk's office. Before we talk about these records, there are some words you need to know.

Deed. The record made of the transfer of property from one person to another.

Real Property. Land and houses are "real" property. All other things we own that can move around with us are called personal property.

Grantor. The person selling the property.

Grantee. The person buying the property.

Witnesses. People who sign the record to confirm that the grantor is transferring the property willingly, that nobody is forcing him to do it.

When a piece of property is sold, the deed is recorded (written into the town record book) so that everyone will know it has been transferred. Towns have lots of legal reasons for doing this. One of them is so that the town can collect taxes from the correct owner. (All people who own property in a town pay a tax on the property to help pay for the cost of running the town.) Since deeds are important legal documents, most towns and counties have taken very good care of them. The deed books usually go all the way back to the beginning of a town or county.

Deeds do not make very interesting reading. They just give the names of the grantor and grantee, tell how much the property is being sold for, and give a legal description of the property. Some of the old legal descriptions can be fun to read, but they don't make much sense to us today. They talk about the property starting at the big oak tree and running by the line of pine trees to the large rock at the southeast corner. When you read some of these, you wonder how people were able to figure out where their property lines were at all. I have included an old deed on page 47 so you can see what one looks like.

Some of the important pieces of genealogical information in a deed can be taken out to save you from copying all the legal language you don't really want or need. This is called making an abstract of a deed, and it means keeping only the important information. You will want to find out the name of the grantor and where he or she lived, the name of the grantee and where he or she lived, the amount of the property (example: 400 acres and a house), the money paid for the property, the date of the sale, and the names of the witnesses. You will also want to list a reference for where you found the deed,

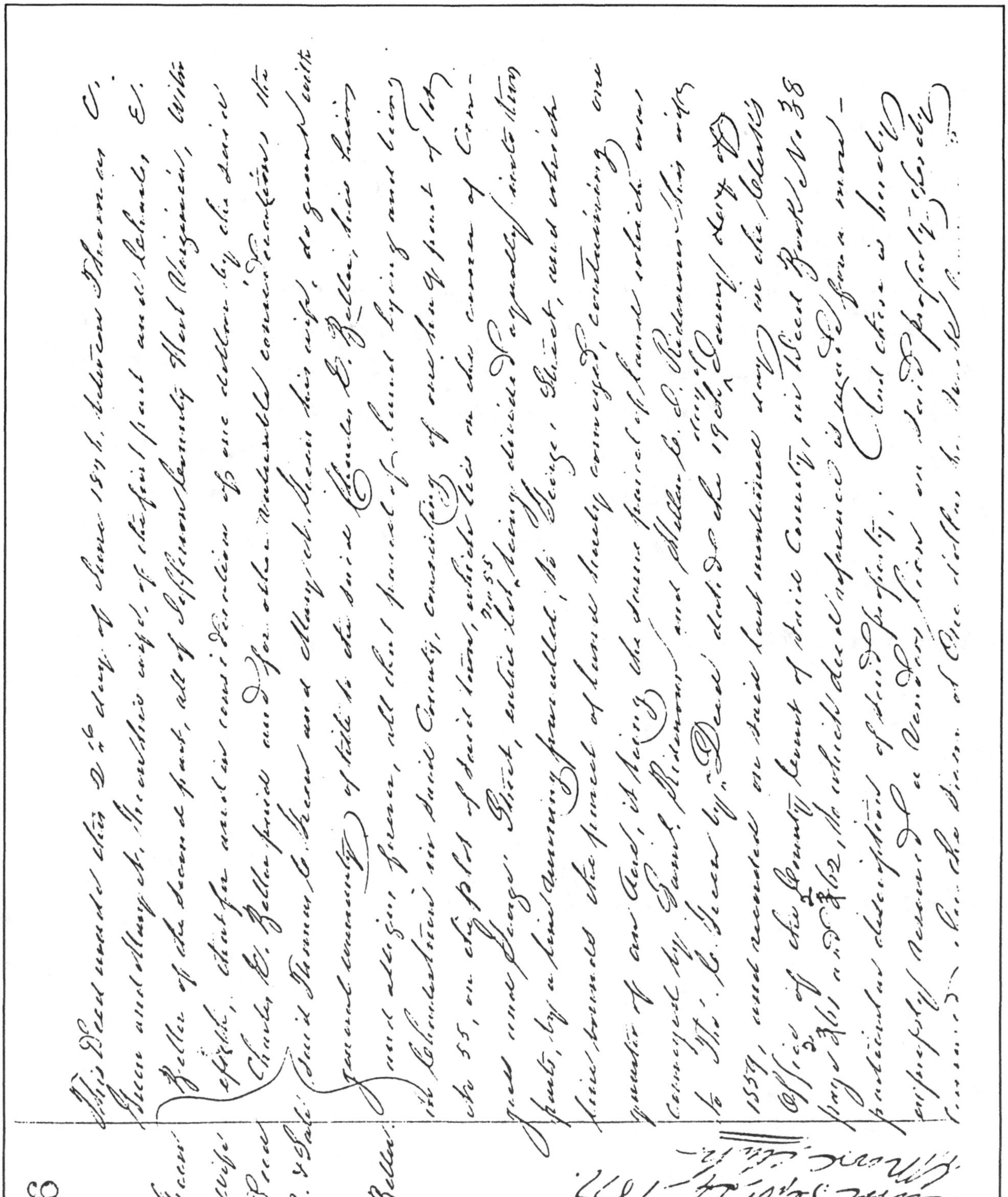

256

Abstract of Deed

County: _Jefferson, W. Va._   Deed Book: _38_   Page: _256_

Name of Grantor: _Thomas C. and Mary N. Green_

Name of Grantee: _Charles E. Beller_

Description of Property: _"All that land lying and being in Charlestown in said county consisting of one ... ? lot No. 55 on the plat of said town which lies on the corner of Congress and George Street, entire lot No. 55 being divided equally into two parts, by a line running parallel to George Street, and which line bounds the parcel of land hereby conveyed, containing one quarter of an acre..."_
24 Sep 1877

Amount Paid: _$1.00_

Witnesses: _can't read_

Legal Description of Property (if names included):

like this: Jefferson County, West Virginia, Deed Book 12, p.141. An abstract of the old deed you just looked at is included on page 48 to show you how it is done.

Now the question is: "How can I use this information?" It does sound like lots of work for something that is not the most useful thing. However, deed records are important because 1) they place a person in a definite place at a definite time, 2) they can give you a person's occupation (farmer, storeowner, blacksmith, etc.), and 3) they were often used by parents to divide their property among their children (which gives you family relationships). A good example of this: I once had a person who was in all of the records in Berkeley County, West Virginia, and then just disappeared. I couldn't find him anymore. Then I found a deed where his wife was the grantor (the seller). She was selling a piece of property that she had received in her father's will after his death. The deed gave the place she lived as Warren County, Kentucky. Suddenly I had found where the family had gone, and I could trace them in those records.

One other point about deed records—some of them have two indexes, one by grantor and one by grantee. If you only look for your ancestor in the grantor index, you will only find times he sold property, and you'll miss the times he bought property. Often you can use the indexes at an online site and not have to go to the town or country to find out whether your ancestor bought or sold land there. But, even if you do find an index listing for your ancestor, the deed records themselves are not likely to be online. You will have to go and find them at the local county or town office.

Will Records

When a person who owns either real or personal property dies, that property has to be divided among the people who should get it (the heirs). Before they die, some people make a document called a will, which explains how they want the things they own divided up. If a person dies without having made a will, the government steps in to decide who should inherit what. The kinds of records that handle dividing up people's property after they die are called probate records. These are also local records. In places with counties, probate records are usually kept in the same place as the vital records and land records. In places where the vital and land records are held by towns, probate records are usually kept at the county clerk's office or by a special probate court.

If the person you are looking for died without a will, you usually will not get very much information from these records. But if the person left a will, you will sometimes find the whole family listed and get all kinds of useful information. The next page shows an abstract of a will for Jacob Beller to give you an example of how much you can find. As you can see, the names of the entire family were listed here, including the daughter's married name and two grandsons' names.

To abstract a will you want to include the following information:

1. Name of the person making the will and the date and place it was made

2. Date and place the will was recorded (wills aren't recorded until after the person dies)

3. Names of each of the persons mentioned and what they received

Abstract of Will

From: Berkeley County, W. Va., Will Book 3, p. 376.

Name of person making will: Jacob Beller

Date and place: 31 Mar 1801, Berkeley County, West Virginia

Date and place probated: 27 Apr 1801, Berkeley County, West Virginia

Bequests:
1. "Well beloved wife Ann" — "one third part of the income of all my lands and living during her natural life."
2. Son, Jacob — 90 acres of land "where he now dwells."
3. Son, Eli — all the unwilled part of my lands when he arrives at the age of 21. Arrange his schooling and guardianship to age 21.
4. Son, Peter — $8 — his land "I have conveyed to him by deed."
5. Son, Isaac — $10
6. Grandson, Abraham — 50 pounds when he comes of age. Also if Eli dies before age 21 or without heirs then "Abraham, son to my daughter Leah shall have one third of the land divided to my son Eli."
7. Daughter, Lydia — $141
8. Daughter, Naomi Sagatha — $141
9. Daughter, Mary Neal — $141
10. Daughter, Leah Morlatt — $141
11. Daughter, Elizabeth Shaw — $141
12. Daughter, Rachel Harper — $141
13. Grandson, William Shaw — $70 when he comes of age

Name of executors: John Vanmetre, Nathan Vanmetre, Captain Jacob Vandoran, Nicholas Straye

Witnesses: John McMurron, John Booine, William Rush, Jacob Vanmetre

4. Name of the executor (the person in charge of doing what the will specifies)

5. Names of the witnesses to the will (must be people who are not receiving anything from the will)

Court Records

The last local records I want to mention here are court records. When people disagree on who owns something or other matters, their disagreements are often settled in court. All court records are kept by the court itself (usually starting with the county level of government). It is worth your time to look in the indexes to court records (if there are any) to see if your ancestor is mentioned. It would be a waste of time to go through individual court record books, since you probably wouldn't find anything. Court records are worth your time only if the records have been indexed. Then you can follow up on anything you find in the index. Some court records are indexed in just one index. Others use two indexes: one for plaintiffs (the person asking for the court action) and one for defendants (the person defending against the action). As with all of the records I've talked about, always find out about the particular system for the place the records are kept so that you do not miss anything.

As I said earlier, these are not records that you will use as often as vital records. But after you have finished with the vital records, it is important to at least check for a will, since if there is one the information will be very helpful. Once you have finished the basics and are starting to fill in background information on your ancestors, you'll find yourself using these local records much more. Each of these records has a possible place in your research, and it's important that you know about all of

them for those times when your research comes to a dead end.

Miscellaneous Local Records

There are three other categories of local records that I want you to know about before we start finding out how to find all these great sources of information. The first are church records. The second are manuscripts or archival records. The third are old newspapers. All of these can be great ways to find more information on your family.

Church Records

In the days before vital records were kept, often the only records of births, marriages, and deaths were in church records. Church records can be hard to find, but they can also be extremely important to your research. In fact, in cases where the vital records are missing, the churches may have the only records available for these events. Many church denominations record baptisms, which in the past usually took place when a child was less than a month old. Most churches record marriages. And many also record burials of their members. In Greene County, Missouri, for example, many of the vital records were lost in a fire. But I have been able to get the information I need on ancestors living there by using church records and old newspapers. Usually the problem with church records is availability. Some denominations (like the Presbyterians) have microfilms of all their old records available, and you can borrow them easily through interlibrary loan. Other denominations (like the Methodists and Catholics) keep their records in the local churches. If that is the case, it is up to the pastor of the local church to decide whether to let you use the records, or whether even to look up the answers for you if you are not allowed to use the records. If, however, copies have been made of church records, they are usually put into genealogical collections.

Manuscripts or Archival Records

These one-of-a-kind materials can be great fun to use. Manuscripts are original material that is donated to a library or historical society to be preserved. Most of these are from famous people whose "papers" are donated. Their papers can include just about anything—old letters, diaries, Bible records, record books about their farms, etc. Other types of archival material include old church records, records of social groups or clubs, maps, and copies of old posters—any original material of historical importance. This type of material can be a good source for information you can't find anywhere else. Lots of this information is being placed on the Internet. Some of this is being done by big libraries, especially university libraries and the Library of Congress, but some local historical societies are doing it as well. For example, the Cayuga County genealogy site has tried to make sure researchers can find out what kind of archival material is available in their area. That is a great gift for researchers.

One of my favorite stories about archival material has to do with Thomas Jefferson, the author of the Declaration of Independence and the third President of the United States. He kept record books (he called them his farm books) about everyone who visited him at his home, Monticello, near Charlottesville, Virginia. When he died his will stated that all of his papers were to go to the new University of Virginia, which he had founded. Because Jefferson was so important, over the years his farm books were printed and indexed. Jefferson wrote down all of the local events in the Charlottesville area, and many people have been able to find information about their ancestors in his farm books that is not in any of the public records. These records are used all the time by historians. Remember, when you are doing genealogical research, you are a historian too!

Newspapers

Newspapers (especially local ones) have all kinds of interesting information in them. Old newspapers are very different from our newspapers today. They are also a lot of fun to read. They are not at all like the other sources we use in doing genealogical research. We always look first for the official documentary records that tell us when a person lived and where. Local histories can give us some idea of what a place was like when our ancestors lived there. But even local histories are written as "history." Because of that, they only talk about the "important" things that happened.

Newspapers are different. They give us a day-by-day or week-by-week look at what it really was like to be living in a certain place at a certain time. Newspapers have all of the gossip and trivia of our ancestors' lives—the things that are not important enough to be a part of history books. When you are doing research, the important thing you will find about using newspapers is that they write about the "ordinary" people, not just the "important" people.

Old newspapers can give you many different kinds of information:

Professional notices: In the times before the telephone and *Yellow Pages*, the only way people like lawyers, doctors, dentists, insurance agents, and land agents could announce their business was in newspapers.

Business advertisements: Let's say that when you research deed records you find that your ancestor owned a store in town. You'll want to look at the old newspapers so that you can see the ads he placed for his business. They weren't big full-page ads like we see in the newspapers today. These were small ads, and many of them make funny reading today.

Public notices: Remember, back before telephones and television, you had to put in the newspaper anything you wanted to announce. So you will find overdue tax lists, lists of people who need to pick up their mail at the post office, notices of church and club meetings, notices for meetings of the volunteer firemen and the militia, and many other kinds of lists.

Public sales: These notices are still in our papers today. They announce sales of estates (wills) or court-ordered sales of property. I once found a public sale for someone who had "disappeared" from the official records in the area. It was an announcement of the public sale of his personal property (property that is not land or house) since he was moving to Indiana.

That gave me the clue I needed to look for him somewhere else.

Personal ads: These include ads for lost-and-found items, places for rent or sale, legal notices, and help-wanted ads. Some of these have information you won't find anywhere else. I once had a client who couldn't figure out her ancestor's occupation. He was listed in the census as a merchant, but when she looked at deed records she couldn't find a store that he owned. I later found him for her while I was looking at old newspapers for something else. He was a merchant who bought and sold slaves.

News articles: In old newspapers there are very few news articles. Some of the ones you will find are well worth reading. They give information that will make your ancestors seem very real. One woman's name appeared in a West Virginia newspaper for sending the editor a radish "which measures two and a half feet in circumference, and weighs eleven and a half pounds" (*Spirit of Jefferson*, 24 December 1850).

Marriage notices and obituaries: These are extremely helpful in places where the public records are missing.

Finding Local Records on the Internet

The last chapter gave you lots of new sources to learn about and made for lots of reading. Now it is time for us to have some fun and actually find and use some of these great sources. In the days before the Internet, there was really only one way to find local records. You had to go to the local town or county office and use the records there.

If you were lucky, someone had made an index to the records and your search could be done quickly. Often, however, you found yourself running your finger down page after page in the record books, hoping to find the name you were looking for.

The arrival of the Internet has changed all of that for at least some researchers. Throughout the country (and, as we will see, around the world) local researchers, county clerks, and others interested in the history of their communities have been working to make the information they have available over the Internet.

We are going to talk about the kinds of research that can be done, using an excellent website that was developed for Cayuga County, New York, as an example. It is important to understand that most

counties have not developed websites that are as complete as this one. I've chosen this one because it shows what can happen to make research that much easier. Again, this is not typical, but it is an example of what you might find if you are lucky.

The genealogy website for Cayuga County, New York, is located at **www. rootsweb.com/~nycayuga/**. Using this one site—and its links to other sites—here is the information you might find (as I did) if you were looking for a family that lived in Cayuga County in the mid- to late 1800s.

Cemetery Records

A lot of volunteers have spent time making lists of cemeteries in Cayuga County, New York. Also, some of the big cemeteries have put records of their burials online. I used the online records for St. Joseph's Cemetery, the major Catholic cemetery for the city of Auburn. Using just those records I could find not only the person I was looking for but other members of the family as well, because the number of the gravesite is listed for each person buried there.

Looking for Maurice Murphy, as I was, I found that there were other Murphys who were buried in the same section and had the same lot number. Sure enough, I found that Maurice's older brother was buried in the same lot. And there was an Esther Murphy in the lot right next to both of the brothers. Using just this one site, I could now travel to the cemetery and find the graves I was looking for and see whether I had indeed found several people from the same family.

Census Records

Other volunteers have been working on indexing federal census records (we will learn about how useful these can be in the next chapter). The entire 1860 census has been indexed and put online here. If you are lucky enough that your relatives lived in one of the smaller towns, you will find indexes for many other years of state and federal censuses for them at this site also.

Church Records

Clicking on this tab at the Cayuga site links you to all of the churches in the Auburn area whose records have been indexed. For some you can find only indexes to marriages. Others have indexes to baptisms of children too. Some have lists of members enrolled in that church in different years, sort of a census of a church. What makes this resource for church records so great is that the indexes are being put online so you can use them from home! As you search around in the records for other places, you will see that this kind of indexing is a rare and special treat for the researcher.

City Directories

In the age before telephone books, big and medium-sized cities often put out a city directory every year. This had a list of everyone living in the city and often gave their occupation also. Usually only the names of the men were given. Once you start to put together who was the father in each family, you can use the directories like a census, seeing where the family lived each year.

Local History and Name Index to Books

Other links lead to a history of the county and to name indexes of county histories that have been done by volunteers. Most genealogical collections have lots of county and local histories for their area. The histories of an area can have a great deal of information. They will tell about the first settlers to reach the area, as well as the early churches, newspapers, and businesses. In each of these histories you will find names from your town, and many times these will be names you can use.

Besides local histories, a good genealogical collection will have lots of books of genealogies of people from your area. People who do research usually try to publish it at some time. Since a lot of their research is done at the genealogical collection in their area, they usually give that library a copy of their research. So making an index of these sources available online, as has been done in Cayuga County, helps researchers find out if they even need to look at the books in the genealogical collection.

Land Records

Revolutionary War Bounty land grants have been indexed and can be found on this website. We will talk about them in our discussion of national records in the next chapter. There are also several tax lists available. Since everyone who owned a home had to pay real estate taxes, these also make a good census of who was living in the county at a certain time.

Maps

About twenty maps have been listed on the Cayuga County website. Some are from the 1700s; others from as recently as 1930. Once I figure out the family's address from the directories, I go right to the map and find where they actually had lived.

Miscellaneous Records

This link leads to those manuscript records we talked about in the last chapter that don't fit the other categories. At this site, there are some interesting finds for researchers. Someone has taken the original pages of the city "minute book" (records of the meetings) and scanned them into files so you can read the originals. Among the other finds are a diary, a list of slaves mentioned in a local newspaper in the early 1800s, an autograph book, an index to the police files from 1912 to 1930, and a list of the names of everyone who worked on a church friendship quilt (with a picture of the quilt) made in 1888. Again, each county will have different treasures among their miscellaneous records. Who knows whether one of them will be by or about your ancestor!

Newspaper Items

This link has some old newspaper articles and an index to old newspaper vital records announcements. You will probably find that old newspapers are among the first things that volunteers like to index, so you may very well find this resource at most of the county sites you will be researching.

School Records

Several old lists of school graduates and graduation photographs can be found at this link. One list dates from 1816, a time period for which records are extremely rare. Someone researching this one document might find the children of a family at a time when there would be no vital records and no names of children mentioned in the census records.

Veterans' Records

If you are interested in military service by citizens of Cayuga County, this site gives you lists of veterans from the French and Indian War to the Vietnam War. This is another popular item for volunteers to index, so be sure to see if there are any for your counties.

Vital Records

Some births and deaths in limited time periods are indexed on this page.

Surname Searchers

Are you interested in who else might be searching for the same name as you are? There is a link that takes you to a list of researchers and the names they are interested in.

Links to Other Sites

Another service provided by this webpage links you with even more information at other sites. For example, there is a link to the Cayuga County Historian's Office, which gives you more information, including the names of families for which they have collected information.

Another link brings you to the Cayuga County Records Management Office and their indexes to petitions for naturalization by immigrants, and to their Civil War bonds index.

Other links bring you to the local historical society and local genealogy groups.

Beller's Law for Genealogy

This list of possible things to look at from just one website gives me a chance to introduce you to the Beller's Law for Genealogy: NEVER pass up a chance to look at an index to anything. I once passed up the chance to look at an index to the 1870 Mortality Schedules for West Virginia. This index had just arrived at my local library in Virginia, and I told the librarian that since I had looked at all the county vital records already, there would be no point in looking at this index. One day the librarian was looking for something else in this index. He happened to come across a death record for someone I had been looking for. I had spent four years looking for this one record. I had missed the person when I searched the vital records at the county clerk's office. The librarian called me immediately with the information. Since then, I have ALWAYS looked at any index I can.

From the Cayuga County website alone, you have access to over one hundred individual indexes. From this one website, working at home, I put together some theories of what I needed to see and how the Murphy family might come together. I did all this before I drove six hours to see the actual records in Auburn, New York. As a result, I arrived in Auburn much better prepared for my visit and got lots more research done while I was there.

Were my guesses all correct? No, but from using this website and all the connections to it, I had gotten done at home at my own computer work that in the old days would have taken me weeks visiting in Auburn.

Even with the right information available on the web, you will still have to go to find some of the information you need. However, you will arrive to do your research much better prepared.

Homework

I know that I said there would be no more homework assignments. However, I hope that by now you will be itching to look at some of the material that might be available about your family. So this would be a good time to stop reading and go exploring on the Internet for some of the counties where your ancestors lived. Take one of the names from your "information needed" sheet and search the web to see what information is available for that county. In a search engine like Google.com, type in the name of the county and state and the words GenWeb. That should bring you to the site for that county. Then have fun exploring what useful information has been made available to researchers.

Kinds of State and National Records

ow that we have seen how to find and use local records, it is time to move up to state and national records and see how they will give us more information for our research.

STATE RECORDS

Let's start with state records. What I am going to say first will sound familiar: The first thing you need to do is find out which records your state has! Each state (just like each county) has different information. What I will talk about here is some of the kinds of records that you might find in most states. Most states have a state archives or state library of some sort. Looking at their website to find out what they have in their collection is a good place to start with your research.

State Censuses

Many states took their own censuses (counts of all the people in the state) in addition to the national census done every ten years. Since these are state records, they are kept someplace within the state, such as the state archives. Most of the really early state censuses (and those taken during colonial times before the Revolutionary War) have been printed as books and can be found in genealogical libraries for your state.

Mortality Schedules

Beginning in 1850, when the national censuses were taken, a special section was added that took information on people who died during the census year. From 1850 to 1880 these censuses, called Mortality Schedules, were collected from the states. The federal government decided to return these schedules to the states in 1919, and most states placed them in their archives. A few states did not, and those schedules are kept at the Daughters of the American Revolution (D.A.R.) Library in Washington, D.C. These schedules have many death records that may not be available in other places. It is worthwhile to look for your family names in the schedules for your ancestor's state.

Vital Records

Most states keep copies of all their modern vital records. Many states have placed copies in their state archives or library of all the microfilms made by The Church of Jesus Christ of Latter-Day Saints of the local records for their state. Many states, like Massachusetts, have also published their very early records in book form so that they can be available everywhere. You will usually find these books wherever your state library collection of genealogical information is kept.

Tax Lists

Some states have on file in their archives their original tax lists back to colonial times. For example, in Virginia (which is a difficult state to research in because of all the lost records) the one very useful set of records available is the Personal Property Tax Lists because the lists go all the way back to early colonial times. Virginia taxed all males over age sixteen, and the yearly lists serve as an annual census. Using these lists, you can trace where people were every single year.

Tax lists may be for land taxes or personal property taxes. Keep in mind that these may be local records in many areas. Remember Beller's Law and at least take a look at them sometime. You won't use them very often, but sometimes they will have the only available piece for your genealogical jigsaw puzzle.

Military Records

We will be looking at military records later in this chapter. These are almost all national records, which are available through the National Archives. But before we became a country, when we were still colonies, each colony had an army, and those military records stayed with each of the colonial governments as they became state governments. In addition to keeping colonial military records, the original states kept records for their militias that fought in the Revolutionary War. Some of the individual states even gave pensions and land grants to people who had served in the militia. If you get your lines back to Revolutionary War times, keep in mind that if you do not find military records in the National Archives, you might still find them in the state archives for the state your ancestor served in the war.

There is one other type of military record that is not national and therefore is not available at the National Archives: the pension records for soldiers who served in the Confederate Army in the Civil War. All of the actual military service records, both Union and Confederate, are held by the National Archives, but people who served in the Confederacy could not get a pension from the federal government later in life if they became ill and could not work. So, individual Confederate states decided to give pensions to their own soldiers. These pension records stayed with the individual southern states. If, in researching an ancestor, you find he served in the Confederate Army from Virginia, for example, it would be worth writing to the Virginia State Archives to see if he ever applied for a pension.

Land Grants and Patents

When we discussed deed records in Chapter 6, I said that there was an earlier kind of land record for an original grant of land to the first owner. These are called land grants and patents. For many of the Midwestern and Western states these are national records, since this land was divided up and given out or sold by various acts of Congress. But for many of the original colonies, these are state records. In colonial times these were called land patents. These are usually well-kept records and can give you information on when your ancestor arrived in an area and where he came from.

Each state had its own system for dividing up the land. Many of these original land grants have been published in book form, giving just the name of the grantee, the size of the grant, and some indication of a grant number. With this information, you are able then to request a copy of the actual grant and its survey. I have a 1750 land grant from the Virginia Northern Neck grants, and I always enjoy reading the closing part about "in the Twenty fourth Year of the Reign of our Sovereign Lord George the Second by the Grace of God of Great Britain France and Ireland King."

Other State Records

Some other groups of records tend to find their way into state archives. These include original church records, collections of Bible records, personal papers of famous people, genealogical notes, and maps. These are the same types of miscellaneous records we talked about in Chapter 6 that were kept locally. Any one of these may have the missing piece to your research—don't pass them by!

NATIONAL RECORDS

National records for the whole of the United States are kept by the National Archives in Washington, D.C. Some of these old records can be very helpful to you in your genealogical research. We will talk about the three major kinds of national records you might be using. These are census records, military records, and immigration records.

Census Records

Vital records are the best way to find out information about family members. But as we saw earlier, the problem is that most places did not keep birth and death records until after the Civil War ended in 1865. Even where the records were kept, they weren't always required until after 1900, so many times we can't find the record we need. For records before the 1860s, the situation is even worse because there are no birth or death records at all for most of the country. We have to rely on will records and hope that all the members of a family have been listed. The one other source that can really help in putting old families together is census records.

When the federal (national) government began counting all the people in the country every ten years (taking a census), it wasn't because it wanted genealogists to have a good source of research today. The U.S. Constitution says that the House of Representatives has to be set up so that everyone is represented fairly and equally. To do this, someone must count all the people and show where they are so that the areas each representative serves have around the same number of people. The way the government does this is by counting every person in the country every ten years. This was done for the first time in 1790 and has been done every ten years since. Each time the census was taken, more questions were asked. The answers to those questions can really help you put together old family groups. The National Archives has an article available online at **www.census.gov/prod/2000pubs/cff-2.pdf** that lists all the questions asked in each of the census years.

You cannot see census records that are less than seventy-two years old. This protects the privacy of the people listed on them who might still be alive today. But you can see the censuses from 1790 all the way to 1930. That gives you fifteen different censuses to use to track down where your family was living and who was part of it. All of these censuses have been put on microfilm, so you look at them by using a microfilm reader. Copies of the censuses are in different places around the country, so you don't have to go to Washington, D.C., to use them. In addition, as we will see in the next chapter, census records are now available in online databases to which you or your library can subscribe.

The first five censuses (1790–1840) did not give much information at all. They can help you find out where a family was at a certain time and how many people were in the family. Then they give the number of males and females in the family by age groups. The censuses that give the best information for doing research on your family tree are the ones from the 1850 census on. Starting in 1850, the name of every person in the family was listed so you can use the census to put your families together. Although what was asked at each census was somewhat different, the most important pieces of information tended to stay the same. You should be able to find the name of every person living in the household, along with their age, sex, where they were born, and their occupation. As the census years passed, more and more questions were asked that give you

information you can use in your research. In 1870 census takers asked whether your parents were born in another country, which would help you know whether the family recently immigrated to the United States.

In 1880 census takers asked for your parents' place of birth, which meant you now could find out where they had emigrated from. That same year, for the first time, every person listed had their relationship to the head of the household given. Now you could tell whether someone living at the house was a niece or nephew rather than the son or daughter of the head of the household. Sometimes you could find the wife's parents living with the family and that would give you her maiden name.

By 1900 the census takers were asking very specific questions about how long people had been married, how many children a woman had given birth to, and how many children were still living. People born outside the United States also had to tell what year they came to the United States.

The 1890 censuses were almost all lost in a fire in 1921 and only exist for 6,160 people living in Alabama, Georgia, and Washington, D.C. Having to go twenty years between the 1880 and 1900 censuses makes you see how important they are for research and makes you wonder what you missed in 1890. When the new census is released after seventy-two years, genealogists rush to be able to bring their family information forward by ten years.

Using the Census Records

The census records can be used at the National Archives in Washington, D.C., and at their regional research libraries. Many state libraries have the census records for their state, so you may not have to go far to see the ones for your state. The Church of Jesus Christ of Latter-day Saints (commonly called the Mormons) have Family History Centers throughout the country. If you have one near you, you can rent census microfilms from their main library in Salt Lake City, Utah, and use them at the Family History Center in your area. The LDS Church has also made the 1880 census available online for searching. In the next chapter we will see where you might find census records online. With the censuses now available through Internet databases, it is much easier than it used to be to use census records. In many cases you can even see the actual census pages online and print out copies for your family history.

The censuses have lots of mistakes in them. We mentioned earlier that records are not always accurate. The censuses are very inaccurate, particularly with people's names. The census takers wrote down what they thought they heard, and sometimes their spelling wasn't too great. Sometimes it wasn't their fault—a person named Mary Anne might be listed as Mary Anne in 1860, but by 1870 her family just called her "Mary" and she is listed that way. Sometimes people gave their nicknames instead of their given names. So using the census records is really like putting together a jigsaw puzzle!

Some of the census takers were also very lazy. Some didn't bother asking all the questions or filling in all the answers very well. Some used ink that has faded so badly that you can't read the writing at all. And the handwriting was often terrible. You may need to use a magnifying glass to decode the writing on the page. But you will find it so much fun that the hardest part will be looking for your own family without stopping to look at all their neighbors on the same page.

Military Records

The National Archives has all the military service and pension records that exist for all the wars before World War I. There are very few records left for the early wars such as the Revolutionary War and the War of 1812, but they are worth looking at when you get your family tree to that point. Most of the records you will find are Muster Rolls and Pay Rolls. On the next page is a copy of some War of 1812 service records for Ephraim Beller, my husband's great-great-grandfather. As you can see, they don't provide very much information. But if you were looking for an unusual name and went to the general index to records from the War of 1812, the record could tell you quite a bit. You would learn, for example, that Ephraim was a corporal; that from August 23, 1814, to September 19, 1814, he was at a camp near Baltimore; and that his home was in Shepherdstown, Virginia, eighty miles from Baltimore. With that information you would have a state and town so you could begin looking for information there. You could also look up history books on the War of 1812 and see if anything interesting happened while your ancestor was serving there.

The really useful military records are the pension records. To receive a pension (money from the government for someone who served in a war and now cannot work himself), the soldier or his widow (for a widow's pension) had to prove his military service. He also had to give some information about himself. If a widow applied to

| *B* | **57**
(Lieut. Col. Mason.)
(Lieut. Col. Minor.) | **Va.**
Militia. | *B* | **57**
(Lieut. Col. Mason.)
(Lieut. Col. Minor.) | **Va.**
Militia. |

Ephraim Beller

Appears with the rank of .....*Cpl*..... on a

Muster Roll

of a Company of Light Infantry Volunteers (who were accepted and received into service for 60 days unless sooner discharged) commanded by Captain Van Bennett, now attached to the 57 Reg't Virginia Militia,

(War of 1812,)

for ....*Aug 23*...., 1814, when took up the line of march, to ....*Sept 19*...., 1814.

Roll dated ....*Camp near Baltimore*...., *Sept 18*, 1814.

Date of commission, ..., 181

Commencement of service, ...*Aug 24*...., 1814.

Expiration of service or } ....*Sept 18*.... 1814
of this muster,

Distance from Baltimore to Shepherds- } ....*75 miles*....
town, their respective homes, after
being discharged,

Present or absent, ...*Present*....

REMARK: Each man belonging to this Co. is allowed 5 days for travelling from Baltimore to Shepherdstown, the distance computed to be 80 miles.

Remarks and alterations since our services were

accepted : ....

....

....

....

....

Ephraim Beller

Appears with the rank of ....*1 Cpl*.... on a

Pay Roll

of a Company of Light Infantry commanded by Capt. Van Bennett, attached to the 57 Reg't Virginia Militia, in service at Baltimore,

(War of 1812,)

for ....*Aug 24 to Sept 23*, 1814.

Roll dated ....

.... *Sept 23*, 1814.

Commencement of service } ....*Aug 24*, 1814
or of this settlement,

Expiration of service or } ....*Sept 23*, 1814
of this settlement,

Term of service charged, ...*1*.... months, *1* days.

Pay per month, ...*10*.... dollars, ... cents.

Amount of pay, ...*10*.... dollars, *24* cents.

Remarks : ....

....

....

....

....

....

receive her husband's pension, she had to show where they were married and give information on their children. Some of these pension applications can give you all sorts of answers. I was researching a Revolutionary War soldier and could not find any service records for him. (Revolutionary War records have a different fire story than all the other records lost in common fires. Most of these records were lost when the British burned the capital in the War of 1812.) I then went to the pension records and found that he had applied for and received a pension. In his pension application I found out that he had fought in the Battle of Fort Washington and was taken prisoner. If a pension record exists, it is definitely worth looking at. So don't give up if you don't find a military service record. Keep looking!

Most of the military service records themselves are available only at the National Archives in Washington, D.C. Most of the indexes and the entire set of pension records for the Revolutionary War are on microfilm, so you can see those at the Regional Archives. The indexes to military records are also searchable through paid genealogy services, which we will look at in the next chapter.

Immigration Records

The immigration records kept at the National Archives are mostly passenger lists for ships arriving in the U.S. from 1819 on. These are very difficult to use because they are arranged by "Port of Entry"—the city where the ship arrived. You could spend forever and not find your ancestors unless you know exactly when they came and where they arrived. If you can locate the record you need, however, what it contains can provide the one key that pulls all your other research together. That happened to me when I was able to finally locate all the siblings in one family by finding them together on a passenger list. With a common name (Murphy), it was my one great chance to sort out all the Murphy cousins in the area and put the right people into the Murphy family I was researching! Fortunately, today there are ways to search passenger lists online, as we will see in the next chapter.

Now that we know what kinds of records we might want to use, let's discuss where we can find these national and state records. At the same time, we can look at some of the best places on the Internet to use these records either from home or from our local library.

Online Searching in Genealogy Databases

In Chapter 7 we looked at how we could locate local records using the Internet. Now it is time to look at where we can find state and national records. The major sources for genealogical records have not changed in the last fifteen years since this book was originally written. What has changed is how much of this information can be found without going to the actual sites themselves. For state records, there is probably going to be one location in each state, either a state library or archives, that will have what you are looking for. The key will be to find that place and find out what parts of its collection might be available to you online. Most likely you will find that indexes have been done to many of the state records. But you will not be able to get the actual record without either writing away for it or going to do the research in person. Just like we saw with local records, however, if you do what work you can online, you can save yourself lots of time and effort when you finally go to do research.

Once you have researched what is available for local and state records, your next step is to access some national data-bases and collections. Since you will probably use the databases online and only visit the major collections later, if at all, let's first look at what you will be able to research from either home or your local library.

Research Databases Online

It used to be hard to talk with kids who had really gotten interested in tracing their family history but who were not old enough to be allowed to research in some of the places that they needed to go to find information. I had to tell them to find an adult willing to go with them and try to get permission for them to do research. These days you are lucky to be able to do so much more research online before you might come to a stopping point like that.

US GenWeb Project

If you haven't already done so, you should take out the list of information you know you need that you made at the end of Chapter 5 and turn on your computer. A whole world of genealogy awaits you! If you know exactly where your ancestors lived, you will be starting your research in the county where they lived through a site like the one we talked about in Chapter 7 for Cayuga County, New York. The site is called a GenWeb and is part of the US GenWeb Project (**www.rootsweb.com/~usgw/**). From this website—which is run by volunteers trying to make as much genealogical information available to everyone for free as they can—you can click on any state to go to its GenWeb site. That site will have links to each of the county GenWebs for the state.

What you will find when you get to the county you are looking for will vary greatly. Some counties, like Cayuga, New York, have fantastic amounts of information, as we saw in Chapter 7. Others have almost nothing available. Since you will probably have ancestors in a wide variety of locations, you will hopefully hit at least some that give you a good start on your research.

RootsWeb.com

The GenWeb project is hosted by RootsWeb (**www.rootsweb.com/**), the free portion of a paid database called Ancestry.com. It is a place that you will also want to visit. It hosts something called World Connect, which is a site where people can upload their genealogical research. You can use it to see whether someone might have researched the same family you are looking for. We will talk in the next chapter about how you must be careful about trusting some of the information you will find here, but it doesn't mean you shouldn't at least see what others have done. Sometimes just seeing where others say the family came from can give you ideas of where to look! This site also hosts mailing lists and message centers that everyone can use to send out questions to

other people researching the same family lines or places that you are.

Ancestry.com

Ancestry.com (**www.ancestry.com/**) is a paid genealogy database service. It can be fairly expensive to get for yourself at home but you can often use it free at your public library or at a Family History Center run by the members of The Church of Jesus Christ of Latter-Day Saints. Searches for a name in this database will often turn up thousands of results. Some will be in census records, others in directories, obituaries, land records, printed marriage records, military records, family or local histories, or newspaper articles. If you are new to genealogy, this can be an overwhelming experience, and it takes lots of time to weed all this information down to the person you are looking for. At the same time, in the area of passenger lists alone, I have used this to solve the Murphy riddle, very much a version of finding a needle in a haystack! I would definitely see if your public library has subscribed to this and only get into this site once you have quite of bit of information already at hand.

Genealogy.com

This paid database (**www.genealogy.com**) is very similar to Ancestry, with indexes of census records, ships' passenger lists, and an extensive library of genealogical materials. It also has access to the Freedmen's Bureau records, a great source for people who are researching African American ancestors. The Freedman's Savings and Trust Company was set up by a presidential order from Abraham Lincoln in 1865 to give former slaves a place to save money. It lasted less than ten years but in that time over 70,000 people registered with the company. Those records contain a lot of information for people who often don't appear in other records.

HeritageQuest Online

HeritageQuest Online (**www.heri tagequestonline.com**/) is another paid genealogy database but has some slightly different records that you can search. In addition to census records, over 20,000 books, and an index of news articles, it includes abstracts of the Revolutionary War Pensions and the Freedman's Bank documents. This site is only accessible at a subscribing library or institution—there are no individual subscribers.

FamilySearch.org

FamilySearch is a website that is run by The Church of Jesus Christ of Latter-Day Saints Family History Library, which we will look at shortly. We have talked about the LDS family research several times already in this book. This is the part of their research that you can use from your own computer at home without having to go to one of their Family History Centers. This site is free for anyone to use and can be found at **www.familysearch.org**/. In addition to the International Genealogical Index, the Pedigree Resource File, and the Ancestral File, which are databases developed by the LDS, you can search many other useful tools at this site, including some census records and the United States Social Security Death Index.

New England Historic Genealogical Society

For those searching for early New England ancestors, this organization has been collecting and indexing material about the earliest settlers of New England for over 150 years. If you are a member of the society, you can access their database at **www.newenglandancestors.**

org. Some libraries also have institutional memberships that you can use to get to this database without having to pay to become a member. It is a fantastic source of information and much easier to access than going through the miles of books on the shelf that you can now search by name on a computer. Among the sources included is *The Great Migration Begins: Immigrants to New England 1620–1633,* which is a wonderful summary of all the information known about the early settlers and their relationships with other families who came to America in the very earliest years of settlement. The database is for all of New England and Canada but is strongest for early Massachusetts, Connecticut, and Rhode Island settlements.

Michigan Genealogical Death Indexing System

Since I just spoke of one regional database, let me mention another one, just to remind you again of how important it is to look locally by county or state to see what may be available for you to use. The Michigan Department of Community Health has made a helpful index available on its website at **www.mdch.state. mi.us/gendisx/search2.htm**. Anyone can use this to search over 170,000 death records for Michigan dating from 1867 to 1884. This is a good example of a state making a wonderful resource available online. What is especially good about this is that it doesn't just give you a name and then make you request the record to get all the information. All the information is right there, including the date of death, age, names of the person's parents, and where the person was born.

US Census Project

A group of people are trying to make every census record in the United States available online for free. This project, which is part of the USGenWeb and is located at **www.us-census.org/**, is an ongoing project so you need to keep checking back to see what has been done for the area you are interested in. When the project is finished it will not offer the real census images the way the paid services like Ancestry do. However, it will offer an index and listing of information for everyone in the census, which has been checked and confirmed to be accurate.

Major Genealogical Collections

Even though your family search may never take you away from home, there are some collections or repositories, as they are called, of genealogical material that you should at least know about. These are the places that hold the actual information that is showing up on those Internet databases like Ancestry.com and FamilySearch.org. Many public libraries and university libraries have developed collections of genealogical material. Historical societies have also strengthened their genealogical collections. But there are four genealogical collections that are very special.

The first (and the largest in the world) is the Family History Library in Salt Lake City, Utah. The Church of Jesus Christ of Latter-day Saints has spent over fifty years going to all parts of the U.S. and numerous other countries making microfilm copies of all the old records they can find. Their members have indexed these records. They have the most complete index to birth, marriage, and death records in the world, and it gets bigger with every passing week. Along with this index they have a fantastic collection of published family genealogies and other secondary

genealogical sources such as local histories. This is the place that every genealogist hopes to visit someday. I finally had my chance to spend a week there in 2004. I would have to say that even after thirty years of research, the library was even more than I had hoped it would be. But you don't have to hurry out and convince your parents that you need a trip to Utah. There are branches of the library (called Family History Centers) throughout the United States where you can pay to rent some of the material from Utah.

Just starting out with their Internet site that we mentioned earlier (**www.familysearch.org**), you will be able to search over one billion names. Talk about never passing up a chance to use an index! The site includes the 1880 census for the United States, the 1881 census for Canada, and the 1881 British census, giving you the chance to check on every person living in those three places. The United States Social Security Death Index is another large database, which can be used along with some of their own databases. No other library in the world comes close to matching this fantastic source of information for your research. As with any genealogy collection, don't expect your search to give you your complete family history. Mixed in with actual entries from vital records are the names entered by other researchers on their family group sheets. The names and information you get will lead you to the real research you need to do to confirm the work that others have done. Your next stop will be the Family History Library Catalog. That will allow you to order the microfilm reels you need so that you can do that actual research.

The remaining three libraries are in the Washington, D.C., area. The first is the Library of Congress, which is the largest library in the United States. The Library of Congress has the best collection of local histories and old newspapers in existence. They also have all the basic genealogical sources that most libraries cannot afford to buy. The only problem with this collection is that it can only be used in the Library of Congress itself. That means that you will need to visit and give yourself lots of time to learn how to use it. If you do get to visit, you will notice that lots more people spend their time in the Local History and Genealogy Room at the computer terminals rather than with the books. That is because this library has subscriptions to all of the major private genealogy services like Ancestry.com and HeritageQuest Online, along with access to the New England Historical and Genealogical Society's online database of early New England history and genealogy.

The third collection is the Daughters of the American Revolution (D.A.R.) Library, also in Washington, D.C. The D.A.R. is made up of women who can prove that they have an ancestor who fought in the Revolutionary War as a patriot. The D.A.R. Library has a fantastic collection of military records and very early records for the first years after the Revolutionary War. These records and books are collected so that people can try to prove their lineage to a Revolutionary patriot. Many of the women who become members of the D.A.R. give copies of their research to the Library, so it also has an excellent collection of published genealogies. The individual D.A.R. chapters are best known for collecting old Bible records and copying the tombstones in cemeteries (especially small family graveyards with only a few stones). They send copies of this information to D.A.R. headquarters in Washington, D.C., so that it can be used by everyone who comes to the library. Their dedication to this work has helped them build a collection of materials different from those found in any other collection. Their library catalog and Genealogical Records Committee National Index are searchable from their website (**www.dar.org/library/default.cfm**). As always, this provides a chance to see whether they have something you need without having to go there!

The fourth genealogical collection is not really one at all. It is the National Archives. Many of the records we have spoken of—the census records, military records, and passenger lists—all belong to the National Archives. It used to be that you needed to visit either the National Archives or one of its regional archives to use these records. In the years that I have been doing research, probably the biggest change I have seen is that the records from the National Archives are the ones most likely to be available through various online services. In fact, using these services you can now look at many passenger lists, all of the censuses, and indexes to military records along with abstracts of the most important documents in pension files without ever having to visit the National Archives.

What To Do Now

All of this information should keep any researcher busy for quite a long time. But I do need to mention a few other things that are accessible using the Internet. They are the message boards and query sites that let you share information with genealogists around the world. It used to be that you could place an ad in a genealogical publication looking for others who were researching your family name. If you were lucky, you would connect with someone and exchange information.

Now you have the opportunity to post online queries on message boards around the world. Through these queries you can find others who are researching the same name and even locate some long lost cousins! Many family reunions have come about because of someone's search for people researching the same family line.

There are also lots of family organizations that have created websites for certain family names, where anyone can post what information they have. Individuals have also done the same thing on their own websites. Often putting in the family name followed by the word *genealogy* in a search engine such as Google can lead to hundreds of "hits" of websites for others researching the same name.

This can be very useful for your research. But it can also be a problem. In the early days of computers, one of the phrases you heard a lot was called GIGO, for Garbage In, Garbage Out. Lots of the stuff that is put online has not been checked. Sometimes accepting what others say can lead to lots of wasted time following information that is wrong, which is why our next section has to talk about evaluating your information and making sure you use the Internet safely.

Evaluating Your Information

When my daughter was born in 1975, she wore a christening dress that had been in my father's family for ninety-five years. The dress came to me with a story. My father's sister had the dress and had used it for the baptisms of her two children. She had been baptized in the dress, as had her father (my grandfather) and his sisters before that. The first to wear the dress was my great-grandmother Angeline. The dress was made for her christening. The story was that Angeline's mother was a Mohawk Indian living in Canada and expecting her first child when a priest came through the area. He convinced her and many others to become Catholics. Since she wanted her baby to be baptized when it was born, she immediately began working on making a christening dress for the baby. The story told how she worked on the dress in the evenings by the fire in the small cabin in which she lived.

There are only two problems with this wonderful story. The first is that the dress itself is machine-sewn. The second is that when I found her marriage record in Canada, it gave her parents' names (and those of her husband's parents). Their parents' marriage records gave parents' names and so on, until both lines traced themselves back to France.

I took the christening dress to a museum textile (cloth) expert, who examined it for me. She told me that the dress does fit the correct time period and that the hand embroidery added to the dress after it was made does match a pattern from the *Godey's Lady Book*. Women would use this book and find patterns they liked and embroider them onto dresses. She also told me that most women could not afford sewing machines when they first came out. But groups of women from churches would buy a machine that they would all share, so there might indeed be a church part of the story after all.

I then talked to a local historian about the French Canadians who came to the United States to work in the mills in Winooski in the 1890s. He told me that there was a time when the new immigrants tended to develop stories of their families—stories that claimed that they were descended from native peoples. My grandfather was born right about the time that those stories were heard the most in

Vermont. Did his mother make up the story to tell him of her own mother? Did he just misunderstand the story she told? I will never know the answer to these questions. But all the questions do not change how I feel about this one family artifact. It is even more precious for me than it was when all I had was the original story. Now I know that there is a mystery to it. I may never know the answer to the mystery. But I do know that this family story is part of the story of how immigrants came to Vermont while still trying to keep their stories of the past.

One of the hardest parts of researching family history is separating out the facts from the stories. One of the most important parts of your research, as we have already said, is those stories. They do not have to be true to be important. Sometimes a story that you find is not true can tell you a lot about what your family was thinking when the story started, which is what happened with the christening dress story. So keep the stories. But if you are trying to be a real historian, make sure you tell as much of the story as you can find out, the parts that are true AND the parts that are not.

This ongoing search to separate the real truth from the stories has always been part of doing family history. In some ways, all of the information available to us on the Internet just makes it harder to keep the stories true. I will give you an example. My husband's Beller line can definitely be traced to a family living in Pennsylvania by 1714. That family is most likely a family that came from the Palatine area of Germany around 1709. If I check online sources, I can see the person who emigrated at that time listed as definitely coming from a place called Schallodenbach, a small village not far from

Kaiserlautern in Germany today. I can just as definitely find this same person listed as coming from Switzerland.

What do you do when you have information that you find doesn't match? Usually you try to contact the people and find out where they got their information. When I contacted the people on this particular Beller, I found that everyone who answered me said they got the information from someone else who said it was accurate.

If you are a researcher who really believes in being a good historian, you will try to be accurate. But you will also recognize that lots of the stuff you will find in other people's research is not correct. That means you need to check the information out yourself. Sometimes you will not find an answer. I have, in the case of this Beller, seen the records from Schallodenbach and they do not go back far enough to let me know if that version of the story is correct.

There have been other times when checking has given me the answer. When I was using that wonderful Cayuga County website before visiting Auburn, New York, to do research, I found several Murphys who were listed in the Naturalization Index for the same date. I guessed that perhaps they were all brothers and went together to the court to say they wanted to be American citizens, even though one of the names, Alexander, was not one I had ever seen mentioned anywhere else in my research. But I started collecting any information on him just in case. I researched him as if he was part of the family.

However, I knew even as I collected information that he might not be. So when I visited Auburn I went to actually see the Declarations of Intent that were signed that day. As it turned out, Maurice and his brothers came to the courthouse with the same sponsors, saying that they had been in the United States for the five years needed. Alexander had different sponsors and had been in the United States for a longer time! Later I would find the ship's passenger list and, as expected, it did not include Alexander. I would also see pages from a special census done in 1840 in Ireland that had the names of all the family members on it. That record showed me that the passenger ship list was correct.

Unfortunately there are some researchers out there who find information in indexes online and just assume connections that are not there. It is important that all this wonderful material that you find be checked to make sure it is correct.

Be a Good Historian!

How can you be a good historian? Let's set up some rules you can use so that you won't get stuck with the wrong information.

1. Collect everything. Get stories from lots of different people and see how the stories match or differ. Go back and ask follow-up questions when you can.

2. Start documenting your stories. Look up census records, for example, that show that the family even lived where the stories say they did. Find any vital records or church records you can. You will still find errors in the records as we have seen, but at least those records are official ones and were reported at the time the events happened.

3. When you find someone in an index on a website, plan on someday checking the actual record to make sure you have the right person. Use the website to get all your information organized before you go and then visit the local offices and check everything yourself.

4. When you've used all the official records, make sure you check all the other sources, like visiting graveyards or reading newspapers. Try to put together the best information that YOU yourself can find. Then you are ready to see what others may have done for the same family name.

5. Check the sources of the information you find on the Internet. If you do an Internet search on a family name, you will sometimes find beautiful, long genealogies that people have written. If they were good historians, you might now not have to do as much work as you might have. But, as good historians, they should be willing to tell you where they got their information so that you can check it out yourself. If they don't want to tell you, be a little bit suspicious and plan on checking the whole thing.

Always share what you know, but also share what you don't know. I had a good conversation with a Certified Genealogist out at the Family History Library in Salt Lake City, Utah. I was trying to decide what to do about writing up that whole thing about the Beller emigration from Germany or Switzerland. She told me something very valuable. She said that a good genealogist writes everything down, shows every source of information, and then comes to the best conclusion that he or she can think of. By showing all the information that he or she found, the next researcher who sees that research will be able to see exactly what was done. If that person has a new piece of information that changes what you did, that's okay! As this professional genealogist told me, "There's nothing wrong with making a mistake in your interpretation if it is based on the best information you can find. The only mistake is saying something without any evidence to back it up."

Research Around the World on Your Computer

When this book was first written, it ended with information on taking a field trip to someplace that would have vital records so that you could learn about researching onsite. There have been so many changes in availability of records that this time the book needs to have something about international research.

It used to be that if you could trace your line back to the country that your ancestors arrived from, that was really good work. If you could find what ship they arrived on, you would add the passenger list to your records, and if you were very lucky, you might have an actual name of a village, town, or city that your ancestor came from. If you were Irish, you probably knew what county in Ireland, as the Irish seemed to pass down that piece of information, at least. But the chances were that your research would end right there. If you were tracing French Canadian lines, you might be lucky enough to get back to an actual parish in France, which was wonderful compared to tracing some other nationalities.

You could, of course, visit your local Family History Center and see if perhaps your ancestor's records had made it into the International Genealogical Index and, again, you might be lucky!

Today, there is no reason to stop at your immigrant ancestor's arrival in the United States. You may still not go back much further as records were not kept that much further back overseas than they were here. But for many of your lines, you just might be able to find enough information so that you can eventually travel to where your ancestors came from and see the world they left behind.

The first part of what I say should sound pretty familiar to you by now. To find out about your ancestors in their home countries you will need to find local records, the same way you do here. Let's first look at how you find out where your ancestor might have lived and then take a look at one county in Ireland that has put together a database of genealogical records that has actually won awards.

Your search begins with the records you have already. Hopefully you have traced your family back to census records that tell what country the ancestor came from. You may even have, from the 1900 census, an idea of what year your ancestor arrived. From census records you will move to ships' passenger lists and try to find out when they came over to the United States. Some of these passenger lists will give you little more than a name and an age. Others will show you whole families traveling together. You will find indexes of passenger lists using services like Ancestry.com if your ancestors came before the 1890s. A free source that is available to search online is **www.castlegarden. org**, which was the arrival station in New York for immigrants from 1830 to 1892. Their database currently has about 10 million names listed of arrivals there, and they have volunteers working to add more names from passenger lists that have not been added already.

If your ancestors arrived in 1892 or later in New York, you will be able to use the records of Ellis Island, the great arrival station for many soon-to-be Americans. The website is **www.ellisisland.org** and a search of its records is free. For each person you locate, you will be able to see the passenger list for the ship they arrived on. You will also be able to see what personal information they provided as they arrived. This might give you the name of the actual city, town, or village they were traveling from.

You will also by now have searched for the family at **www.familysearch. org**, the website sponsored by the LDS Family History Library in Utah, to see if any vital records might exist for your ancestor. If he came from Canada or Great Britain, you probably have also searched the 1881 census from those two countries that is available on the same site.

Let's say then that you have found a likely town or county or department (in France), or canton (in Switzerland), etc.

for your ancestor. Now it is time to think local again. The same kind of GenWeb that we saw for the United States has been set up in other countries also. For each country you can access their national site, and then keep clicking on smaller and smaller areas until you get where you want to search. Ireland's site (**www.ire landgenweb.com**) is divided by counties and then often by baronies and/or civil parishes within the counties. The French GenWeb (**www.francegenweb.org**) is divided by Départements and Régions and, as you would expect, is written in French. What you have is a WorldGenWeb with individual countries linking themselves to it. Some are made for the researchers of that country, and therefore you need to understand the language. Other sites have access in English to their records. Germany does this, for example, and German records can be accessed through Rootsweb here in the United States (**www. rootsweb.com/~wggerman/**). As with the states that are part of the USGenWeb, the amount of information included can vary a lot!

We will use County Clare, Ireland, as an example of a very good website for research in another country. County Clare is one of the famine counties, the parts of Ireland hit hardest by the potato famine in the 1850s. Millions of Irish left their native country and dispersed to the United States or Australia during what is often called "The Great Hunger."

That means that there are lots of people trying to find information about where their ancestors lived before coming to America. Starting at the Ireland GenWeb and selecting County Clare, the list of resources with information includes the County Clare Library, and a link takes you to their website. I have used this site myself online, corresponded with the librarians there with questions, and then researched there in person in 2005.

Irish records are scarce before the late 1860s. They are even more scarce if your ancestors are Catholic Irish. The wealthier Anglo-Irish who were part of the nobility can trace their ancestors back for generations. The poorer Catholics are not so lucky. However, the Clare Library has pulled together whatever records do exist for the area and has volunteers indexing all of them.

The best records for tracing individual Irish leaseholders is through what are called the Tithe Applotment Books of the 1820–1840 time period and Griffith's Valuation of 1855. Both have been indexed for County Clare. Most of the census records for Ireland from the 1800s either burned during a fire at the Public Records Office in 1922 or were destroyed by the government. But the existing census for 1901 has been indexed and can be searched at this site. If a townland within a parish has records, they also have been indexed and can be searched at the site.

I was researching the small Killofin Parish and was able to find history and photos for the parish and the census and land records I mentioned before, along with a list of school teachers in 1824! A neighboring parish actually had a database of church records beginning in 1852 searchable on the website. Using the information from this one site, by the time I went over to actually see the maps and originals of the land records, I had been able to narrow my search down to just a few families with the common names of Breen and O'Brien who lived in the area. Because of this, I was able to spend time walking the roads of Lakyle North (which had only eleven families in 1901) and

reading headstones in the nearby graveyard, instead of spending all my time in the library.

Have Fun, but Search Safely!

The other thing that the Internet gives you as a researcher is the chance to ask questions of other researchers. It was leaving a message on an Irish genealogy query board that gave my husband and I the chance to go on an ultimate field trip! All the research we have talked about so far has been in databases. Anyone can search in these online. You don't ever have contact with other researchers using these databases. The message boards are different. Here you are sending out a request for information from other researchers. Most times your requests will not even be answered. I have posted dozens of queries over the years and probably had answers from other researchers on fewer than ten of my queries.

If you are going to post queries, it would be good to have a grown-up check out the site and then make sure they also see any answers you get from researchers. Just the same as you are taught about surfing the Internet for other uses, you need to remember basic safety rules. Never give out your name and address, for example. Genealogy researchers are great people. But, especially if you are a young researcher, remember all the things you have been taught already about safety on the Internet. And then you can enjoy your research!

We have gone all around the world on our search for records. Unlike in the days before the Internet, we can now do lots of research from home or our local library. That research will probably keep you busy for many years. At times it will seem that you will turn on your computer and find tons of information. Other times you will spend hours and find nothing. But you will know to come back and look again sometime, to see if maybe the new indexing done by researchers or the information posted by someone else holds the puzzle piece you need to make your story more complete. From that research you will have a fun hobby, but perhaps also a great excuse to travel back and see where those people from your past came from. Researching your family tree can lead to some wonderful field trips!

IRELAND

The Ultimate Field Trip

On a drizzly day in September 2005, what the Irish call a "soft" day, my husband and I walked the ground where his Murphy ancestors had walked 160 years before. The story of how we got to Davidstown, County Kildare, Ireland, is a good way to show how all of your time and effort and research can come together.

The Murphys were a difficult line to research because the name is such a common one. In addition, the Murphy ancestor had died a few years after arriving in the United States, leaving a widow with three small children. She had taken the children away from Auburn, New York, to be closer to her own family in Missouri. So the children had not grown up knowing that much about their father's family. The information that had come down the generations about him was very sparse.

It was my research in Auburn, Cayuga County, New York, that gave me the information to put the family together. Starting with only Maurice and the fact that he had several siblings, including a sister named Susan and a brother named Thomas, I used online cemetery and church records to find two more siblings, Michael

and Esther. Having some more unusual names to go with the very common Murphy, I began searching passenger lists for Esther, Susan, and Maurice and got very lucky! By the time I actually went to Auburn to fill in details, I pretty much had the family. All I needed now was a townland in Ireland to take them back to. The name I needed was waiting for me on both Michael's and Esther's gravestones—they came from Davidstown, County Kildare, Ireland.

Davidstown was so small it wasn't even on the map! The nearest town was Castledermot. And there was little information available online for County Kildare. But there was a query board where I could list what I knew and hope that someone who could help would read it. Someone did! An Irish researcher named Michael Wall had become fascinated with the fact that such a high proportion of people from one parish in County Kildare, Castledermot, had ended up in Auburn, New York. When he saw my query about a family from Davidstown who had moved to Auburn, he answered it with the information that Davidstown was part of Castledermont parish. He and I began exchanging information, not just on the Murphys but also on some other Castledermot families. I could get access to the church records for Holy Family Church in Auburn, New York. He could search out the Griffith's Valuation for the land records and maps of the area. And he had access to a simple document, called Scully's Census, that named all the members of the families in Castledermot Parish in 1840. We exchanged information back and forth for the next several months.

Finally, my husband and I decided we wanted to actually walk the land his family had come from and planned a trip to Ireland. Michael Wall took the day off, and we met at his home in County Carlow. On that "soft" day we hiked the family property (property that had actually remained in one branch of the family until 1958). Then we visited the local landmarks, the cemetery where Maurice's father was most likely buried, and the church where the Murphy children were baptized. It was a special day, and not just because we walked on land that family had walked on over 150 years ago. It was special, too, because we walked that land with a descendant of someone who would have been a neighbor. Michael Wall's ancestors had also lived in Castledermot. Descendants of two Castledermot families had gotten together for the first time in 150 years.

This is just one story I could tell you that came out of my years of genealogical research. My research has gained me friends in France, Ireland, and Canada. But some of the stories did not require going that far away. Not long ago, my husband and I stood for a while in front of the home in which his father had grown up. My husband had grown up not ten miles

away but had never been there. As he remembered stories his father had told him about growing up, it was as if his father lived again. His father was gone, but the stories survived!

Putting the Jigsaw Puzzle Together

Hopefully you have completed the exercises in the early part of this book. If you haven't already done so, spend some time now checking out some of the databases on the Internet that we've talked about in the last half of the book. From here you should be able to move on with your research and see how far it can take you. Eventually you may find yourself visiting the places where your ancestors used to live. Perhaps you will be able to follow their steps all the way back home to the country from which they originated. Whether you can do this or not, you will have learned about their lives through your research and may feel that you have made part of the journey with them.

You will certainly not complete all of your family lines. There will be some dead ends—people for whom the jigsaw puzzle pieces may never be found. That will be discouraging. I have some lines that I have been researching for over thirty-five years, and I know that I will probably never find the information I need on these. Hopefully, you've found some lines that just seem to run back on their own. One young student of mine researching in Vermont vital records suddenly found a string of marriages that not only finished her five-generation chart but also sent her two generations further back!

Genealogy has its ups and downs. If you think that you will be able to find everything and wrap up all your research in six months or a year, then this is not the hobby for you. Sometimes I have gone years without finding anything new on certain lines. But I have not given up—after all these years I've learned that you need to be stubborn and determined. I work on other lines in the meantime and make progress with those.

Genealogy is not for everybody. There is a lot of detail work involved, and some of the research can get boring. However, even completing the first five generations and preserving family stories for that time period is a reasonable goal for anyone to achieve. Beyond that, the search for more records is for those who truly have the desire to make it a lifelong hobby. Whatever you do, please do not throw out any of the research you have done while working through this book. What you have done is history. Put it aside if you want. Then, twenty or thirty years from now, when the urge to find out more comes back (and it will!), you will have a head start and will have preserved some stories of people who may be long dead by then.

Whether you keep researching now, leave off where you are, or come back to it later, remember that you are unique and the collection of stories in your history is special to you. Good luck in putting together your family jigsaw puzzle, and most of all have fun with it! Use your research as an opportunity to make those ancestors of yours have a chance to live again in memory.

Appendices

Family Group Sheet Number: _____

Husband: _____

	Date	Place	Source
Birth:			
Marriage:			
Death:			

Occupation:	Military Service:
Church:	Other Marriages:
Father:	Mother:

Wife: _____

	Date	Place	Source
Birth:			
Marriage:			
Death:			

Occupation:	
Church:	Other Marriages:
Father:	Mother:

Children (Start with oldest):

Name	Birth	Marriage	Spouse	Death

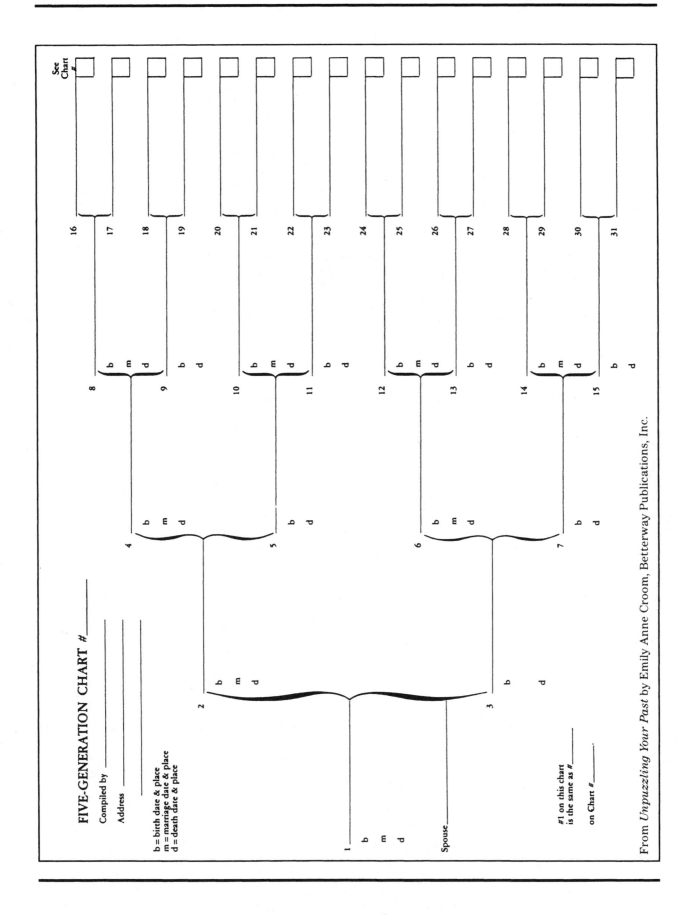

FIVE-GENERATION CHART #

Compiled by

Address

b = birth date & place
m = marriage date & place
d = death date & place

From *Unpuzzling Your Past* by Emily Anne Croom, Betterway Publications, Inc.

Abstract of Deed

County: Deed Book: Page:

Name of Grantor:

Name of Grantee:

Description of Property:

Amount Paid:

Witnesses:

Legal Description of Property (if names included):

Abstract of Will

Name of person making will:

Date and place:

Date and place probated:

Bequests:

Name of executors:

Witnesses:

Resources for Researching Your Family

Forms, Charts, and Information

You can find free family group sheets and pedigree charts at:

www.rootsweb.com

www.familysearch.org

You can find a listing of what questions were asked in each United States Census at:

www.census.gov/prod/2000pubs/cff-2.pdf.

Free Genealogical Databases

www.rootsweb.com. This is a free site provided by Ancestry.com, which contains many useful databases and message boards used by genealogical researchers.

www.us-census.org. The GenWeb Census Project which links to all online indexed census material.

www.rootsweb.com/~usgw. The home site for the entire USGenWeb project. You can access every state and county GenWeb from this home page to find out what databases they have put online about their locality.

www.castlegarden.org. A free database with the names of over 10 million persons who arrived in New York City from 1830 to 1892.

www.ellisisland.org. A free database of arrivals at Ellis Island from 1892 on.

www.dar.org/library/default.cfm. This Daughters of the American Revolution Library site includes an index to the genealogical records compiled over the years by members of the organization.

Paid Genealogical Databases

Each of these sites requires payment to access their databases. However, many public libraries have subscriptions to at least one of these sites so that you can access their information for free there.

www.ancestry.com

www.genealogy.com

www.heritagequestonline.com

www.newenglandancestors.org

GenWeb Sites for Some Commonly Researched Foreign Countries
(with websites in English—most others also have websites but they are not in English)

World GenWeb home website: **www.worldgenweb.org/**

Britain: **www.britishislesgenweb.org**

Canada: **www.rootsweb.com/~canwgw/**

France: **www.francegenweb.org**

Germany: **www.rootsweb.com/~wggerman/**

Ireland: **www.irelandgenweb.com**

Italy: **www.italywgw.org**

Mexico: **www.rootsweb.com/~mexwgw/**

Norway: **www.rootsweb.com/~wgnorway/**

Poland: **www.rootsweb.com/~polwgw/polandgen.html**

Russia: **www.rootsweb.com/~ruswgw/**

Sweden: **www.rootsweb.com/~swewgw/**

Other Genealogy Books for Young Readers

Taylor, Maureen. *Through the Eyes of Your Ancestors*. New York: Houghton Mifflin Co., 1999.

Workman, Ira. *Climbing Your Family Tree: Online and Off-Line Genealogy for Kids*. New York: Workman Publishing Co., Inc., 2002.

Yerkow, Lila Perl. *The Great Ancestor Hunt: The Fun of Finding Out Who You Are*. New York: Clarion Books, 1990.

Index